The Spiritual MBA:

Discover How to

Manage Your Biggest Asset

Vladimira Juskova, M. Ed., MBA

Copyright Page

The Spiritual MBA: Discover How to Manage Your Biggest Asset

By Vladimira Juskova, M.Ed., MBA

Copyright 2018 Vladimira Juskova. All rights reserved.

ISBN: 978-1-9994942-2-3

No part of this publication may be reproduced, stored in a retrieval system, or transmitted in any form or by any means, whether electronic, mechanical, photocopying, scanning, auditory, graphic, without written permission of the author, except in the case of brief excerpts used in critical articles and reviews. Unauthorized reproduction of this work is illegal and is punishable by law.

Because of the dynamic nature of the Internet, any web addresses or links contained in this book may have changed since publication and may no longer be valid. The views expressed in this work are solely those of the author.

License Notes

This book is licensed for your personal enjoyment only. This book may not be re-sold or given away to other people. If you would like to share this book with another person, please purchase an additional copy for each recipient.

If you are reading this book and didn't purchase it or it was not purchased for your use only, then please return to your favorite book retailer and purchase your own copy. Thank you for respecting the hard work of this author.

Limit of Liability & Disclaimer Page

While the publisher and author have used their best efforts to ensure that the information in this book is correct at press time, they make no representations or warranties with respect to the accuracy or completeness of the contents of this book and do not assume any liability to any party for any loss, damage, or disruption caused by errors or omissions, whether such errors result from negligence, accident, or any other cause. Neither the publisher nor the author shall be liable for any loss of profit or other commercial damages, including but not limited to special, incidental, consequential, or other damages.

The advice and strategies contained herein may not be suitable for your situation. The author/publisher is not engaged in rendering professional services, and you should consult with a professional where appropriate. This book is not intended in any way to offer any medical advice. Examples given are provided strictly for illustrative purposes.

Dedication

To my inspiration, my love, business partner, a serial entrepreneur and most importantly my soulmate Warren Backman! I am eternally grateful to be able to share this remarkable life journey with you!

To the Universe! Thank you for the inspiration!

And most importantly to YOU, the reader!

***

The need and a nascent readiness for a new and more spiritually-inspired, holistic and all-encompassing approach to building a life of lasting wealth and happiness is what ignited the spark that led to the creation of this book.

It is my sincere wish that you enjoy it and gain from it!

To you, the Spirit within you and the boundless opportunities ahead!

The Spiritual MBA

***

Personal Motto

MAY THIS BOOK **INSPIRE** YOU TO BE…

*

"The **GREATEST VERSION**

of the **GRANDEST VISION** that

YOU HAVE for **YOURSELF**"!

**

~David Cameron Gikandi~

***

Table of Contents

Preface………………………………………....	10
Introduction…………………………………….	14
Spirituality & Business Belong………………..	25
Spirituality & Wealth Creation………………...	30
I Promise: What's in It for You……………….	33
Time for Some Spiritual Poetry………………..	43
A Dream of an 11-Year Old…………………...	44
From Education to Dedication………………....	46
What We Are All After………………………..	51
The Iceberg Theory of Wealth Creation……….	58
The Evolution of Consciousness…………….....	63
The Spiritual-MBA Way or Spiritual-Preneurship	71
New Thought and the Mind Stuff…………..….	79
The Untold Story of the Brain………………....	81
Let's Get Meta-Physical…………………….....	92
Secrets About Your Subconscious……………..	94
The Not-So-Strange Secret…………………....	101
Desire is the First Law of Gain………………...	103
Harnessing the Power: Focus & Concentration....	108
Unlocking the Law of Attraction……………...	116
The Spiritual-MBA Toolkit…………………....	126
Karmic Giving & Gratitude…………………....	129

The Magic of Believing…………………………..	133
Detachment: If You Love It, Set It Free………….	137
Dollars-Want-Me Mentality………………………...	140
Know Your Wealth Creation Profile………………	143
What Spiritual-Preneurs Really Do………………...	145
Grab Good Habits, Kick the Bad Ones……………	148
Leverage the Now………………………………..	151
Ride the Idea-Wave: Inspired Creation…………..	157
Let Life Happen…………………………………	164
From SMART Goals to Hypnotic Intentions……..	166
Follow the Ball Through…………………………	174
What Winners Actually Do…………………….....	179
The C+3P Equals Success Momentum………….....	183
Mind Expansion and Your Path to Fulfillment……	186
Don't Just Team-Build but also Dream-Build…….	192
Wealth-Creation Ritual: Visualized Meditation…...	197
Command Your Built-In Success Mechanism…….	202
The Prosperity Game: Step into the Flow………...	209
Your Three Musketeers…………………………...	213
Can You Hear Your Spiritual Self? ………………	220
Overcoming Resistance and Allowing……………	225
Mind Sync and Energetic Integrity……………….	235
Clear Your Energy Through Tapping…………….	242
The Emotional Freedom Technique………………	253
Forgive the Hawaiian Way……………………….	255

From Corporate to Spiritual Law	263
The Spiritual and Success Law Convergence	266
What Are You Here to Do?	269
The Life-Path System	271
From Chaos to Clarity	275
Conclusion	280
Acknowledgements	284
About the Author	285
Appendix A: Bibliography	287
Appendix B: Relevant Trivia	294
Appendix C: Success-Building Affirmations	296
Appendix D: Tapping for Specific Issues	300
Appendix E: Energy Points: Meridians	301
Appendix F: Map of Consciousness	302
Appendix G: Maslow's Hierarchy of Needs	303
Connect with Me	304
Success Trigger Page	305
The End	306

Preface

The Spiritual MBA?

Did the title catch you off guard? The truth is, there is a new movement emerging across the globe that aims to integrate more spiritually-rooted values and spiritually-inspired principles into everyday life, including the workplace and business at large. As Corrine McLaughlin, the founder and Executive Director of the Centre for Visionary Leadership observes:

> **"There is a growing number of business people who want their spirituality to be more than just faith and belief—they want it to be PRACTICAL and APPLIED".**

To this point, Professor Ian Mitroff, and the author of *A Spiritual Audit of Corporate America* claims that "spirituality could be seen as the ultimate competitive advantage". A *USA Weekend* poll reported "that 47% of Americans consider spirituality the most important element in their happiness and they want to bring this spirituality to all aspects of their lives, including their work".

An article published in *The Sloan Management Review*, a research magazine of MIT Sloan School of Management, concluded that "people are hungry for ways in which to practice their spirituality in the workplace. The word 'spirituality' is used generically and seems to emphasize how one's beliefs are applied to the day-to-day, rather than 'religion', which can invoke fears of dogmatism or exclusivity" (McLaughlin).

Ideas around the concept of a Spiritual MBA or a 'spiritual-preneur' have been incubating in my mind for a while. With the emergence of a new narrative and an increased degree of acceptance of spirituality in business, I felt the time was right to give my ideas "wings" and capture this new spiritual wave that is penetrating even the 'impenetrable' business world.

What is spirituality in business? The definitions and interpretations are many and still forging. The spiritual MBA book is the first of its kind life-success reference book that lays out a new spiritually-inspired self-leadership framework. This framework, if applied, builds a strong foundation for a new wealth-creation and happiness paradigm. Most importantly, this book introduces you to an entire toolkit of unique and spiritually-inspired success-building strategies and nuggets of wisdom that you are not likely to pick up in a traditional classroom and that you can easily leverage to your advantage!

The importance of spirituality in business is undeniable. I am convinced and have personally witnessed the benefits of spiritually-inspired approaches. The global management consulting firm McKinsey & Company (Australia) found that "productivity improved, and turnover was generally reduced when companies engaged in programs that use spiritual techniques for their employees". For instance, prayer and meditation are two spiritual techniques that have already infiltrated the corporate setting. McKinsey & Company further remarked that many companies have already built designated mediation rooms. Other new spiritual practices, such as visualization, deep listening, and intuitive guidance, are also taking root.

On that note, welcome to the *Spiritual MBA Development Series*! The first volume of this exciting new venture sets out a new spiritual approach to self-leadership and provides unique strategies that will help you better manage your biggest asset: your mind! While most of you may be familiar with the concept of an infopreneur, I will introduce a new 'genre' of entrepreneurship that is called for: a spiritually-inspired entrepreneurship or 'spiritual-preneurship' and with that a new phenomenon- spiritual-preneur! Spiritual-preneurship is a new self-leadership framework, a new way of being, a global online community, and a new platform to promote, share and lead by example. You can judge for yourself, however, I am of the view that the spiritual-preneurship approach has the potential to create more sustainable and rewarding outcomes as it focuses on building value from within. In short, the *Spiritual MBA* book is a roadmap that makes spirituality more applied and pragmatic. View the various strategies and techniques discussed throughout as your success levers and you will certainly benefit!

So, without any further ado!

***

Introduction

A recent scroll through the Instagram home-page brought me to this:

"You are the lead actor, director, writer and producer in the movie of your life. If you do not like an aspect of it, change your story"!

Re-write! Re-create! Re-design! Are you ready?

A new blockbuster is hitting the theatres near you called *Incredible Life*! An accurate depiction of your life and where your current trajectory will bring you. Based on a true story, sensational reviews, unbelievable acting! Starring: YOU! Did I get your attention? Now let's see that movie!

Close your eyes, fast-forward and IMAGINE what your life is going to be like in 5 years. Imagine what it is going to be like if you do not change a thing; if you live your tomorrow exactly the same way you lived your yesterday. Same thoughts, same views, same way of looking at yourself and the world, same habits, same level of awareness. What is the picture that you see?

Above all, do you like the picture you see, or does it scare you a bit? If the answer is yes, you are not alone!

In the words of an American poet and philosopher Henry David Thoreau, "the mass of men lead lives of quiet desperation". Despite our big dreams, startling ambitions and unrestrained optimism, somehow, we get lost on our individual journeys. We wake up one day and frightenedly realize that our life has become what Earl Nightingale calls the "composite average of the averages". Have you experienced one of those mornings? I must admit, I have!

As Zig Ziglar, a well-known American motivational author observes, most of us dream of becoming "meaningful specifics" but we somehow end up living our lives as 'wandering generalities". We tend to forget that occasional failures and roadblocks are all a necessary part of our life journey. Rather than see them as temporary, we regard them as definite and this belief leads us to develop a somewhat defeatist mindset that leads to stagnation or self-sabotage. After a few unsuccessful experiences, many of use plainly give up and settle for the life we don't really like and particularly, the one that we are not meant to live. We shrink our dreams, or stop dreaming all together and little by little, we compromise on what and where we shouldn't and unwillingly resign to living a life of confirmed desperation and our happiness and success remain elusive.

What about the future then? The irony is that many of us expect our tomorrow to be better than yesterday, yet, we show very little willingness to change our ways. We keep going about our life the same way, with little or no awareness of our self-imposed limitations. Clinical practitioners define this as insanity; doing the same things over and over, while expecting different outcomes. I am not implying that we are insane. I do, however, agree with the author and psychology Professor Daniel Ariely and his observation that people are "predictably irrational" and act in predictably irrational ways, even when it comes to their deepest aspirations and living the life of their dreams.

Now, let's go back to our movie. An OPPORTUNITTY to see a …

MOVIE Re-MAKE! Starring the NEW YOU!

It is September 2022 and you are returning from a fun-filled family vacation in Europe. Your 4th vacation this year! Your mortgage is paid off, in fact, you are financially independent. You love what you do and are fully present and aware in each moment. Your life is full of blissful moments and you let it unfold effortlessly and with the outmost faith as you actively participate in its co-creation. You look again and realize that you suddenly have and are everything that you have ever imagined for yourself and those close to you!

Robust health, passionate relationships, effective and fruitful business partnerships, lucrative business opportunities, loyal and fun friends, supporting family, global travel, star-like fame, global reputation, new innovative business ideas, philanthropic work, your own legacy, whatever YOU choose to pursue and whatever personally drives you and fulfills you on a daily basis! All the "niceties", all the luxury, all the toys and gadgets, all the homes, all the clothes, shoes, watches, all the opportunities to make a tangible and significant difference in the world! You name it! Whatever your greatest vision for yourself was, you are now living it! You feel that you are living the dream! Or at least, you are living the LIFE of your DREAMS or what I call a 'life by design'. And if you are wondering, yes, it is possible to live one! YOU are the architect of the destiny that you seek so aim high! And remember:

"Nothing is impossible, the word itself says I'M POSSIBLE"!

~Audrey Hepburn~

You are walking down the street and suddenly stop in front of a bookstore. A vision from the past blasts through your mind, a déjà vu of sorts triggered by a book you spot on display: The *Spiritual MBA* Volume 3. The book sends you down memory lane! You start remembering where you were in your life and how much you have grown and accomplished since you discovered this self-development series and its first volume. You are proud of all your remarkable accomplishments and all the changes you made and are forever grateful to your friend who recommended this new life success reference book spotted in a bookstore window. You now know that your friend handed you a very special gift. A master key that unlocked the path to a NEW YOU: a stronger, happier, wealthier and more fulfilled you!

That very key is now in YOUR hands and it is up to you to decide how you want to use it and what next step to take! May the following statement by Nido R. Qubein be a reminder of your true power and serves as an inspiration on your personal journey.

> "The most of history's greatest achievements have been accomplished not by the most talented, but by the people who were willing to take on greater risks and challenges and see them through".

***

A Moment of Inspiration

The *Spiritual MBA* book is a result of an inspired action taken by an enlightened entrepreneur. Yes, I do walk the talk so when an intuitive nudge came knocking on my door, I answered. It took me about three months of focused effort and boundless joy to create this practical handbook. Since it is a self-help book, I recommend reading it in 20-minute increments. This is the recommended optimal reading time so that you absorb and retain the most out of the material at hand, while keeping your attention up. To this point, it has been proven in multiple studies that after about fifteen minutes of focused attention, our mind takes so called 'mini-vacations'. Do not let these mini-trips spoil the value of your reading and set some uninterrupted time aside for your self-development!

The inspiration and the content of this book draws on my personal experiences as a business (MBA) graduate, a successful female entrepreneur and a spiritually-minded person! I firmly believe it is mind over matter! The invisible before the visible, with the Spirit being the foundation. I was born an entrepreneur at heart and that is the direction I took after I earned my MBA. My entrepreneurial journey started in 2012 when I joined my partner Warren, a remarkable visionary and a successful serial entrepreneur of his own, to pursue a new business opportunity. I joined a newly formed advisory firm with projects focused on the commodities sector, namely a few mining projects in South America. My experiences along the way lead me to create my own success philosophy that is partly rooted in spirituality. My view: have one foot firmly on the ground, and allow for the other one to stretch, expand and be tested for a more rounded and holistic view.

As the saying goes, 'birds of a feather flock together' and spiritually-inspired entrepreneurs attract similar types. An entire book could be written on the value of social support networks, online communities and the importance of building your social capital at large.

Needless to say, the more I interacted with other accomplished entrepreneurs and business executives and learned about their fascinating paths to success, I found something I was not expecting to find! A pattern started to jump out and became more and more pronounced over the years. I came to realize that many of these 'mega-successes' were more spiritual than I would have thought and certainly more spiritual than I was at the time. I have to admit; my formal education did not train me to expect to see much co-mingling of spirituality and the world of business. Even courses on entrepreneurship were few-and-far between. Do you see where I am going with this? My conversations with these successful, spiritually-driven and extremely self-aware entrepreneurs made me curious. I began to gradually immerse myself into a new field of study, which became a passionate and a growing interest of mine. My readings focused on areas of spirituality, metaphysics, New Thought, neuro-linguistic programming, numerology, energetic healing etc. As someone once said to me:

"When the student is ready, the teacher will appear"!

And my spiritual teachers and business mentors definitely showed up! With every step and every question, the universe would reveal a new resource, a new expert, a new technique, a new remarkable mentor.

Over time, my new interest evolved into a healthy obsession: testing my new knowledge and looking for a new and more spiritually-inspired way to building a life of boundless wealth and happiness. After all, my own self-development journey made me realize that "we are spiritual beings having a human experience" and not the other way around (Deepak Chopra). That is, we are not just physical three-dimensional human beings who happen to have the odd spiritual experience. We are Spirits to begin with and our Spirit is our inner strength, voice and foundation. A bit of a crazy thought at first, especially to the scientific crowd, but ask around and you may be surprised at the diversity of beliefs you'll find! So, who is to stay?

Interestingly, as my knowledge grew, so did my repertoire of tools, tips and strategies. The various business and personal challenges I encountered while building the advisory business served as an impetus to look for more innovative and effective strategies to get to the finish line. I'll be honest. No one's success journey is void of challenges and neither was mine. I confess, at times I felt I needed all the help I could get! As I began to internalize my newfound knowledge and started integrating it into my everyday life, this new way of living became the way. My new success-building beliefs, habits and mindsets were deeply embedded and automatic. From a learning standpoint, I reached the level of unconscious competence, but we will get to that. What's more important to note is that as I began to view and live life through a more spiritual lens. And the more I did, the more I began to realize that the only fulfilling way to build and live a happy and abundant life, at least for me personally, is to do it the spiritually-inspired way! And this starts by building value from within! The proposed spiritual-preneurship among other things is a self-leadership framework. It is an approach that can be integrated into any sort of undertaking, whether personal or professional. It is applied, pragmatic and effective.

Combining my business acumen with a spiritual approach led me to discover a series of spiritually-inspired tools and principles. These in turn helped me build a solid wealth foundation, which resulted in incredible breakthroughs in both my personal and professional life. Parts of the road were treacherous, as I said. But the more I lived the concepts and I detached from wanting to see and live the final outcome, the more noticeable and progressive the results were. All of a sudden, the smaller wins turned into giant leaps of progress and average opportunities turned into lifechangers! The inherent tension that I had felt between spirituality and business suddenly dissipated and I knew this was the only satisfying way forward. I also knew I had to share my story to inspire and encourage others to follow a success recipe that has been tested.

It took me 3 years to earn an MBA from a reputable business school while working full-time to support myself. It took another 5+ years to upgrade my education to a spiritual one! My view: I earned an honorary spiritual degree granted by the universe that accelerated my success and gave me the perfect recipe to build a fulfilling, abundant and happy life. Due to the tremendous transformational power that some of this newfound knowledge had on my life, I felt a burning desire to share it with those who are looking to grow and actively pursue their dreams. I hope that my story inspires and that this book becomes an important stepping stone to a more fulfilling life or a renewed vision that you have for yourself. May this book and its strategies serve as your 'success parachute' that will catapult you to astonishing heights of accomplishments, because that is what you deserve!

***

Spirituality & Business Belong

We live in a digital age and our lives have literally gone online! With one easy click of a button, mountains of information are at your fingertips. As you Google spirituality and business these days, you will see that a new narrative is emerging on this subject.

Is there a place for spirituality in business? The truth is, I've been nurturing a desire to write this book for a few years now. But then the rational mind set in, started to over-analyze and subtle doubts overshadowed my creative idea. Are the more traditional segments of this world, such as the business world, ready to open itself to the ancient spiritual wisdom and higher laws and principles that govern this universe and constitute the building blocks of our physical reality? As these pages were being composed, an interestingly serendipitous blog was printed in the *Huffington Post*. Similar to my beliefs, experiences and conclusions, the author of the article Suzanne West remarks:

"Spirituality is likely not something that is chatted about in the boardrooms around the world. […] the corporate world has fallen into a myopic trap that has left out all the extraordinary assistance that

spirituality can bring to the vitality, prosperity and longevity of businesses.

I believe spirituality has been unfairly dismissed because it is incorrectly associated as a synonym for religion. Spirituality is a universal concept, that is the domain of no one, as it has no divisions, claims or separations. Spirituality is a natural part of who we are and therefore belongs not only in business, but in our communities and countries".

***

I am happy to observe that we are starting to awaken to this reality at a collective level. Nonetheless, please allow me to nudge you along the spiritual continuum! Perhaps the one area in business where the concept of spirituality managed to gain a stronger foothold is entrepreneurship. This is mainly due to the fact that entrepreneurs are perceived by many as visionaries and creators and builders of businesses. But, as Suzanne West remarks, the term spirituality implies that we are all meant to be 'active co-creators' of our lives. In other words, the act of creating and crafting a winning vision is not just a task left to the entrepreneurial and the artistic types. Quite the contrary, we are all creators of our own reality! We are the architects of our destinies;

or the executive producers and creative directors of our *Incredible Life* movie. But, to succeed at this creative endeavor, we have to first realize a few things about ourselves. This include an accurate understanding of the nature and scope of our power and how to harness it and use it creatively to our advantage. As you discover your true nature and become more aware of the power that lies within you, you will suddenly see that your key priority is to learn how to effectively manage it and put it to a constructive use. This is the focus of the first volume of the *Spiritual MBA* development series.

A central premise in our discussion worth repeating at the outset is that the only way fully rewarding way to build lasting success, wealth and happiness is to build it with a spiritually-inspired approach or the spiritual-MBA way! This because the spiritually-inspired way leads to self-realization, which is our ultimate goal, and requires that we share our unique gifts and talents with the world, while making a positive contribution. From what I have seen, the non-spiritual way often leads to short-lived earnings, sporadic moments of abundance and elusive happiness. We can all name examples of businesses or people who thought of themselves as above law. We can all think of people and businesses who didn't play by the higher principles only to find themselves in a sticky situation later.

The spiritual-MBA way creates more sustainable outcomes because it forces us to act in alignment with broader spiritual principles that govern the universe. As the article in the *Huffington Post* further explains:

"The businesses that recognize the power of the spirit in their companies will not only survive but thrive in today's context".

The spiritual-MBA way creates more win-win scenarios for all parties involved as it is rooted in the spirit of collaboration and an integrative rather than a competitive mindset. Spiritual-preneurs have recognized this distinction and approach their life, work projects, partnerships and relationships with the very same mindset. Let me illustrate so that the you grasp the essence of this approach.

IMAGINE that you are negotiating with someone over something that you want, let's say a commission fee. Now visualize this 'thing' as a big pie of your choice. For the sake of argument, there are three parties negotiating. At the end of the exercise, you have to divide the pie among the three stakeholder groups based on the outcomes of the negotiation. How would you go about this negotiation and how would you divide the pie? As most, you would probably first assume that the size of the pie is fixed, which lends itself to an erroneous conclusion or perception that the more one party gets, the less there is for the other two. This may seem to be true, but it is not how spiritual-preneurs think and act. Spiritual-preneurs are focused on finding ways to enhance the value (pie) that is on the table first. They are motivated to find creative ways to enlarge the pie so that the final value created is greater than the perceived size of the initial pie. Spiritual-preneurs are focused on identifying hidden value and untapped potential. Their approach ensures that at the end of the day, more was created and there is more to divide, which leads to everyone walking away with a bigger slice.

Why is such a rewarding negotiating outcome even plausible? Spiritual-preneurs are more intuitive and self-aware and realize that what they seek to gain from a transaction is not necessarily what the other party may want. Their approach requires an honest inquiry and total transparency, among other things. This integrative approach that is inherent to the spiritual-MBA way is known in the world of negotiations as an integrative bargaining (Roger Fisher et al). It is a collaborative approach that leads to more creative solutions, with each participant capturing greater and more personally meaningful value out of a transaction (interaction, project, negotiation, partnership, join venture etc.). The spiritual-MBA way has the potential to bring about greater and more satisfying outcomes than more traditional linear approaches because it is more inclusive and focused on creating multiple wins, each crafted based on the respective values and priorities of each party (entity) involved. This is what I call 'priceless spirituality'.

***

Spirituality & Wealth Creation

My second message and a deep personal conviction is that there is absolutely nothing wrong with focusing your efforts on wealth creation and tapping into spirituality and the life force in you to create financial wealth. Due to societal conditioning, we often view spirituality and financial wealth creation (making money) as somewhat opposed. This goes back to our limited perception of spirituality that often equates it with religion. Ironically, this was my initial perception. Having grown up in a communist country where even thinking about spirituality was a taboo, my early associations and perceptions of spirituality were limited to religious studies and a few monasteries I visited on my trips throughout Europe.

On the topic of financial wealth as a motivator, we all know that we can make a more substantial and long-lasting impact on those around us and the world if we have financial resources, money, call it what you wish. The truth remains, the more financial wealth we create, the bigger the impact that we can make. The bigger the legacy that we can create! An acquaintance of mine once said: "Your life can be divided into three phases. Building your skills (learning), making money and giving back"! While money is not the only way to contribute, very little tangible good can be achieved without it. Therefore, our efforts need to be focused also on building financial wealth. To this point, an American New Thought writer and author of *The Science of Getting Rich*, Wallace Wattles, elaborates:

"Whatever may be said in praise of poverty, the fact remains that it is not possible to live a really complete or successful life unless one is rich. No man can rise to his greatest possible height in talent or soul development unless he has plenty of money; for

to unfold the soul and to develop talent, he must have many things to use, and he cannot have these things unless he has money to buy them with".

**

So why limit yourself? Let the Spirit within you guide you on your way to building the life of your dreams. Give yourself permission to live the abundance and affluence that you are meant to live. Build your wealth foundation, build your wealth and build the world around you by giving back in tangible and transformative ways!

As you read and absorb the information on the pages that follow, you may be prompted to examine your current views and beliefs. Your beliefs are the result of your physical heredity and years and years of social conditioning by the context of your environment, such as your culture, family customs, schooling, international experiences, social circles, social media etc. As you go through life, you encounter challenges and are faced with roadblocks that often force you to look within, re-examine and re-adjust. Keep an open mind as you read this book. At times, we realize that our beliefs became outdated and need to be recalibrated, so to speak. This book may prompt some of you to realize that you have lost sight of your goal completely. Or, you may suddenly realize that you are pursuing the wrong one; a goal that was not defined by you and does not align with your higher purpose. Keep track of these aha-moments that surface as you go along. I encourage you to have a notebook ready so that you can jot down any insightful observations on your self-development journey. Are you ready? Let's walk through some fundamentals, but first...

***

I Promise or What's in it for You

Give me one minute and I will show you how this 'life-success' companion will directly benefit you.

First, it is a time-saver and time is money. The information compiled in this book has been distilled from several years of readings, focused study, observation and experimentation. I am grateful to be able to share it with you at this very moment. Throughout this book, I introduce you to various experts and point to outside resources that you may not have otherwise discovered on your own. Only those strategies and techniques that proved themselves most effective went into the creation of this success reference book. The thought-provoking and action-inspiring material that you are holding in your hands has the potential to jolt you out of your comfy couch if procrastination is your enemy. The book was designed to first and foremost inspire, while making you aware of your own spirituality and boundless power. This is what you can expect to gain from the time investment you are about to make. You will learn how to:

MANAGE YOUR BIGGEST ASSET

You will learn how your mind actually works. You will be exposed to some ancient wisdom, life-changing success principles and new tools that will help you train and leverage this invaluable asset of yours. A well-trained mind is your pathway to freedom and living a life that you choose for yourself. A happy, healthy, wealthy, abundant & fulfilling life!

SYNC YOUR TWO MINDS

You will learn about mind-sync and why it matters! I will also introduce you to some powerful tools to harmonize your conscious and subconscious mind. See how you can put an end to self-sabotaging behavior that leads to an unsatisfying existence! You can achieve more if you decide to do so and have access to the right set of tools. This is what the spiritual MBA toolkit is all about.

RE-PROGRAM YOUR MIND

This book will introduce you to specific techniques that will help you clear your mind and your energetic field from anything negative that may be weighing you down. You will discover new tactics to consciously program your mind for success, health, wealth, and happiness instead of unconsciously allowing your mind to operate in a mere survival mode. I will show you how to cultivate a winning mindset and ride the success momentum.

FOCUS YOUR MIND

We will talk about the power of a committed long-term focus on your goals and the importance of the right success habits. You will learn how to give your conscious mind some time off and tap into your intuitive side. A distinguishing feature in my life coaching work is the integration of a life-path system, which we will get to. The value of this system is undeniable! It provides a shockingly accurate focus lens that illuminates a specific set of challenges that each of us need to individually overcome on our journey to living a successful and fulfilling life.

EXPAND YOUR MIND (consciousness – imagination - beliefs)

The material in this book will expand and challenge what you know and currently think about business, spirituality or yourself. It will bring new insights into how your mind really works and will make you see that there is a Higher view, which we all are a part of. To fully benefit from this book, allow yourself to have your beliefs challenged and your views 'upgraded'.

LEAD YOURSELF TO SUCCESS

Irrespective of your field of expertise or personal aspirations, the most important person that you will ever have to lead is yourself. This book discusses some powerful self-leadership tactics and success habits that are all part of the spiritual MBA toolkit. This toolbox is your roadmap to working more effectively and living more enjoyably and abundantly! As Suzanne West rightly observes:

"The industrial revolution did a bit of disservice to business by turning human beings into 'workers' and taking joy and happiness out of the 'working

life' equation". The industrial revolution is over, but we still manage certain companies and their employees as if they worked on a factory production line".

DRAW OUT YOUR INNER POWER

This material will make you more aware of the limitless creative power that rests within each of us, including you. The techniques shared herein will help you discover and get in touch with your intuitive and spiritual Self. By the time you get to the end of the book, you will know how to tap into your inner reservoir of power, inspiration and creativity. You will see that your journey and any 'life development' work starts within.

Are you looking for more proof? The very term 'education' is derived from the Latin verb 'educare', which means to 'draw from within'. It is my sincere WISH that this book will inspire, empower and motivate you. I hope it educates, entertains and awakens your soul! I hope it nudges you to kickstart a new constructive habit or becomes a call to action on something that you have been neglecting! Ultimately, I hope that it leads you and guides you onto a rewarding journey of self-development and self-discovery. This book gives you a roadmap to self-realization. How you use is completely up to you! All I have to say to you before we proceed is this:

"Seize the day"!

***

What Others are Saying

Beta readers of the pre-launch version of this book described it as "an entertaining, insightful, informative and a practical guide to a better and more fulfilling life". They also appreciated the "unique voice and perspective of a female entrepreneur and the book's reality value, as it draws on first-hand experiences in both my business and personal life. Insightful new information and practical strategies are interwoven with personal success stories, 'aha' moments and testimonials. The anecdotal evidence is there to increase your belief in the effectiveness of this material. Take my story as tangible proof! Or, to quote an old family friend and a mentor:

"Do what I did, and you will have what I have"!

In 2002, an article ran in a local newspaper in the Niagara peninsula with the following headline: "Parents sacrifice for their kids' education"! The article profiled a story of a recent graduate, a recipient of the Dean's Gold Metal, and a newcomer to Canada who earned herself a $100,000 scholarship to a graduate program at an Ivy league school. Can you guess what I am about to tell you next? Yes, that story is about me! That was 16 years ago and only 4 years after my family moved to Canada. Since then, I spent about $100,000 on my education, which gave me three post-graduate degrees, including an MBA in Global Business and Entrepreneurship. Nonetheless, some of the most valuable information and insights came to me outside of the classroom, and a lot of them have been included in this book. In a period of 5 months after I started working with the principles and strategies discussed, I left my 9-5 job, incorporated my first company and met the man of my dreams and my business partner! I firmly believe that:

"You can make a living 9am-5pm, but you can make a FORTUNE 5pm-9am"!

Over the past four years, our advisory company managed to carve itself a sizeable share in a highly lucrative and tight industry that was almost impossible to penetrate. At least to an ex-ballet dancer born in former Czechoslovakia who got inspired by the

American dream and decided to become a woman of influence and a role model to other aspiring leaders and mainly the youth. But that is a story for another time and another book, as building the commodities business is an endeavor that took a tremendous amount of time and resources. It is true that nothing worthwhile in life comes fast and easy! Needless to say, my business goals and ventures I took on as an entrepreneur allowed me to travel the world, which has always been at the top of my list. Since 2012, I literally flew around the globe twice and visited about 200 places. At least that is what my Facebook history has recorded! Not bad for a girl who grew up in a small European town about 160km north of Budapest.

I feel grateful and blessed to be able to say that I am living a life that I consciously designed, that integrates the Higher view and allows me to reach for bigger and bigger dreams. I am my own boss and while I work harder than I have ever worked at any other job, I experience joy, abundance and happiness on a daily basis. I wake up energized and approach each day with positive anticipation and excitement. Unless this is your daily reality, maybe you have something to learn from my story and the information we are about to discuss.

Even if it is just one useful trick or a piece of information.

As you may have guessed, I was not born with a silver spoon in my mouth. My personal and professional trajectory brought many unexpected turns, curve balls and challenges that I had to overcome. My cumulative experiences made me who I am and led me to this point. These gave me lessons, insights and new perspectives that I draw on and that inform my decision-making process. Most importantly, these experiences made me see my true power that emerged in moments of great disappointment and temporary defeat. My triumphs reinforced my belief in my abilities and kept me going. I say this:

If education teaches one, it is dedication that makes one!

And dedicated I remained! I chose the unbeaten path and did what many others would not be willing to do. At this point in time, I have a desire to leave a tangible spiritually-inspired legacy behind. This starts with the creation of the *Spiritual-MBA* development series and the spiritual-preneurship framework.

The principles and tools discussed in this book work if you work them. They certainly guided me on my way to a happier life and a fuller pocket! I urge you to start testing these concepts and experimenting with them in your own life, while working through your own set of challenges. We all have something to work through, so you are not alone! You have probably heard once before that knowledge is power only if it is used. I therefore invite you to put this knowledge to a productive and fruitful use! Let me repeat at the outset that the most effective and lasting way to achieve your desired outcomes and transform your life is by first working on yourself. I personally started to witness the biggest growth and experienced great fulfillment the moment I stopped focusing so much on the final outcome and rather focused on becoming the greatest version of the grandest vision that I had for myself (Gikandi). The outer rewards came when the inner value was built.

What about you? Are you living the life of your dreams? Do you have a clear vision of your dream-life would be like or are you missing one? Or even worse, have you given up on one all together? To get your imagination going, let me inspire you with some spiritual poetry!

Time for Some Spiritual Poetry

Did I not mention this book was unlike any other? Since I like to share anything that makes me happy, I have copied below a favorite poem of mine called *Invictus* or *The Unconquerable.* It was written by an English poet and a critic of the Victorian area, William Ernest Henley. Even if poetry is not your thing, I am confident that its deeper message will resonate and empower. It will also to neutralize your mind so that it is better prepared to receive any new incoming information.

The unconquerable

Out of the night that covers me,
Black as the pit from pole to pole,
I thank whatever gods may be
For my unconquerable soul.

In the fell clutch of circumstance
I have not winced nor cried aloud.
Under the bludgeonings of chance
My head is bloody, but unbowed.

Beyond this place of wrath and tears
Looms but the Horror of the shade,

And yet the menace of the years
Finds and shall find me unafraid.

It matters not how strait the gate,
How charged with punishments the scroll,
I am the MASTER of my fate,
I am the CAPTAIN of my soul.
~William Ernest Henley~

Are you the captain of your Soul?

***

A Dream of an 11-Year Old

I've come to realize that there are only a few moments that stand out in our mind with razor-sharp clarity decades after they occur. That fall Saturday afternoon at my uncle's in my native country Slovakia is one of those moments. My parents had a wedding to attend so they put me and my brother up with our Uncle Jarko. We both adore him to this day!

Jarko always had an entrepreneurial streak in him, and that is one of the reasons I gravitated toward him. He is my favorite uncle to this day. It is with an amazing clarity that I remember Jarko telling me a story of his friend's daughter marrying a guy from Germany and moving abroad.

Living abroad?! What a foreign, yet intriguing concept for an eleven-year old girl who knew nothing but her communist environment she grew up in and she tried to rebel against. She recalled with the same clarity the story of her mother's friend who moved to the USA shortly after the Berlin Wall came down in 1989. These stories turned into sprouting seeds of an early desire that planted themselves deep in the little girl's consciousness and eventually turned into a borderline-obsession. A burning desire that, years later, would send her entire family on a daring move overseas!

You guessed right! That little girl was me. I was 11 when the wall in East Germany came down and Slovakia opened itself up to the West. To show that where you begin in life has no impact on how high you can climb, I was 14 when I got my first pair of real jeans from a neighboring city of Budapest! My mom's family lives close to Hungary and to this day, I remember making occasional shopping trips to the Hungarian flea market, or north of the border to Poland for a special Polish caramel candy called krowki.

It is only years later, looking back at my life with a deeper understanding of Self and the universe, that I fully realize what my childhood dream may have co-created. I am convinced to this day that it was my obsession or burning desire to live abroad that was partially responsible for moving my immediate family across the Atlantic about seven years later.

***

From Education to Dedication

My new life in Canada began some twenty years ago, or in 1997 to be precise. Time flies! Both me and my brother were allowed to pack two suitcases of our most precious personal items and some clothes. When I arrived, I opened a checking account with $2,000. That was over 60,000 in Slovakian crowns! I paid my undergraduate tuition from money earned from five part-time jobs.

Since then, my life took me down a remarkable and adventurous path! I invested in myself, earned a few graduate degrees and twenty years later, I am an accomplished entrepreneur, a global businesswoman, a spiritual-preneur, a life coach, an author and the list does not stop here! However, I am most grateful to be able to share my story to inspire you and show you that if I did it, so can you!

For the sake of context and some history, I spent the first 10 years of my professional life doing leadership development work at the Rotman School of Management (Rotman) at the University of Toronto. This work was in line with my life-long interest in learning and education and in helping others grow and develop. I also was fortunate to have found myself at the right place at the right time, meeting the right people or mentors that enhanced my growth and facilitated my upward movement. Or perhaps my willingness to learn and grow brought these mentors to me.

Nevertheless, as strong as my aspirations to move and establish myself abroad once was, so was my desire to build and run my own company. I turned this desire into a goal, put a plan together and enrolled in a Master of Business Administration program at Rotman. For my readers outside of Canada, Rotman is affiliated with the University of Toronto (UofT), which is Canada's premier research and teaching university. In 2018, U of T moved up to the 23rd place in a prestigious global university ranking that pooled 500 universities from a list of 1500. While about two thirds of most business graduates choose to pursue banking or management consulting careers upon graduation, I had my eyes set on a different prize: the less beaten, uncertain, but exciting path of an entrepreneur!

The MBA program gave me a solid business foundation and provided me with a blueprint and key management and leadership tools and mindsets that I was going to need in my entrepreneurial toolkit. Although Rotman still offered very few courses on entrepreneurship, a course in Organizational Psychology focused on organizational alignment introduced me to the concept of a 'can-do' mindset and self-efficacy. It was taught by one of the best in their field, Professor Gary Latham. To his day, I remember his stories about the famous boxer Muhammed Ali and his positive self-talk that he practiced daily to reinforce his self-image and build a can-do mindset. I began to do the same. In fact, positive self-talk was one of the first success-building habits that I picked up and cultivated. Specifically, every night, I would remind myself of three things I did well that day. A powerful routine! As the universe would have it, Gary's organizational psychology course paved a way to a new field of study I was about to discover, but let's not jump ahead. If you are in the field of management, I highly recommend reading Gary's latest book titled

Becoming an Evidence-Based Manager: Making the Science of Management Work for You!

STAGES OF COMPETENCE BUILDING

As I began to internalize new information and insights about self and the universe, I began to notice more significant breakthroughs occurring in my life. There were some bumps along the way, but I viewed them as learning opportunities. As Tony Robbins claims, it is not what happens to us that matters, it is the meaning that we assign to what happens that frames how we interpret the event. That is what makes us or breaks us. In this sense, a tragedy to one person may be nothing but a little hiccup to someone else. It is all a matter of perspective and the choices we make.

Over time, persistence paved its way to victory, in both physical (tangible or financial) and spiritual terms. My inner work paid off and what was once a new concept, belief, or a technique was now running at the level of unconscious competence. If you are not yet familiar, I invite you to review the four stages of competence building that we all go through when developing a new skill, whether it is driving, cooking or learning a second language, or any other skill.

The **First** Stage: Unconscious Incompetence. You don't know that you don't know.

The **Second** Stage: Conscious Incompetence. You know that you don't know.

The **Third** Stage: Conscious Competence: You know what to do but have to think about each step.

The **Fourth** Stage: Unconscious Competence. Your newly acquired knowledge and skillset have become second nature.

Think of when you decided to take up golfing, tennis, piano or any other activity. Your first few attempts at any new activity were probably unsuccessful; you may have been clumsy, cautious and a bit unsure. You probably kept mentally rehearsing whatever instructions you received prior to beginning. As you may know, the quickest way to move along the competence continuum is through dedicated and deliberate practice. With practice, your new skill becomes second nature and you showcase it with confidence. How long should you practice? We will get to that. The real secret, however, is do the RIGHT things long enough and consistently.

This is when you reap the biggest benefits and see your life unfold as you envision it to. And what are 'right' things? They are the subject of this book. Are you ready?

What Are We All After?

The wisdom and tools shared in this book have the potential to bridge the gap between where you stand in life and your 'self-actualized' you. Self-realization or self-fulfillment is achieved through the deployment of our unique gifts and talents! And that is what we are ultimately all after. Let me explain.

In 1943, a renowned American psychologist Abraham Maslow proposed a *"Theory of Human Motivation"*, which included a hierarchy of needs. Please refer to Appendix G for a visual diagram. According to Maslow's theory, people are motivated by three distinct groups of needs: basic needs, psychological needs and self-fulfillment needs. As it is a hierarchy, we need to meet our basic needs first (these include shelter, food, clothing) before we can move up a level and start addressing our psychological needs, such as our need for friends, family, self-esteem and a feeling of accomplishment. Once our psychological needs are met, we are ready to move on to the final category of self-fulfillment needs, which include self-actualization and achieving one's full potential, including the pursuit of creative activities.

***

Success is About Whom you Become

As you know by now, my key objective in creating this reference book was to inspire you and give you the tools to help you build an even more successful, happier and wealthier life than the one you are living at this very moment! Let's spend a few minutes defining this at times elusive concept.

What is SUCCESS? And what does it mean to you personally? Have you reached the level of success that you had imagined for yourself? Or are success and happiness still elusive and ephemeral, lasting for only a short period of time and then they suddenly fade away or vanish completely? Now let me ask you this. If you have reached the desired level of success, how do you hold on to it? And what do you with yourself next? We see many people go from rags to riches but also the opposite direction; falling from the ranks of the rich and becoming borderline broke. Many lottery winners or even professional athletes end up in a dire financial state only a few years following their big payouts. I raise these questions to encourage you to take a minute to think about them, as otherwise you would not.

As a matter of fact, I repeat my earlier suggestion and invite you to read this book with a piece of paper or a journal in front of you so that you can jot down your observations or insights to these questions as we move along. You'd be surprised at how valuable your notes may turn out to be months or even years later.

Irrespective of where you currently stand in life, this book came to you as a reminder that:

"You are BORN to WIN! You are DESIGNED for ACCOMPLISHMENT!

You are ENGINEERED for SUCCCESS!

You are ENDOWED with the seeds of GREATNESS"!

~ Zig Ziglar~

Be sure to read at least one book by Zig Ziglar, another well-known American author and an icon in the field of human motivation and achievement. In both his writing and teaching, Ziglar reminds us of this greatness that resides within us, but that we forgot about on our evolutionary path. So, let me remind you that among other things, you are a beautiful powerful spiritual being meant to live an abundant, happy and successful life! Repeat this affirmation daily to anchor this vision deep within your subconscious. Say to yourself daily:

"Abundance is the condition of my life"!

Let's now to our discussion of success. As subjective and personal as it may be, there is a floating commonly accepted definition of success out there. Success is defined as a "progressive realization of a worthwhile ideal" (Earl Nightingale). Earl was a famous American author and radio speaker, who spoke on the subject of human character development, motivation and meaningful existence. On the outside, success could mean being a good parent or starting your own company, because that is what you have always dreamed of doing. Achieving success is really about pursuing and staying committed to your passion despite the external world not always supporting you or telling you to choose a more conventional path, for more conventional and linear reasons. If you are like me, you are probably drawn to success stories resulting from people taking unordinary, challenging and at times risky paths that paid were adventurous and also brought high success dividends. After all, it's all about calculated risks and everyone's risk appetite is different.

As you may already know, success is about the journey, not the destination. Success is about committing to a process of life-long development and doing what it takes daily to become the "greatest version of the grandest vision" that you have for yourself. The financial wealth follows your inner wealth. Formulating this new and improved vision of yourself is your principle responsibility, especially if you wish to join the ranks of other accomplished leaders and successful preneurs.

Our discussion of success would not be complete without mentioning Napoleon Hill, another American success and achievement celebrity-author of the 19th. In fact, Napoleon's most known self-help and success book, *Think and Grow Rich,* is placed on the curriculum of many private schools in North America. If you have not read it, treat yourself to this masterpiece! Did you know that more people became self-made millionaires because of the *Think and Grow Rich* book than any other book ever published? This is what I call insightful trivia!

The story of Napoleon Hill is a peculiar one. He was hired by Andrew Carnegie, a wealthy American industrialist of the Gilded Age, to dedicate a significant part of his professional life to the study of the principles of success. This meant interviewing and observing self-made millionaires of his era, such as Henry Ford, Thomas A. Edison or Charles M. Schwab. Carnegie asked Napoleon to synthesize and distill his findings into a philosophy of success. This became his second famous publication titled *The Law of Success in 16 Lessons*. I highly recommend that you put some time aside for this 600-page publication. I can almost guarantee that you will be drawn to read it more than once, as was I.

After about two decades of a detailed examination of success, I certainly think we all have something to learn from Napoleon Hill. For him like for many others, success is not about the end-result. Rather, it is about whom you become on your journey and as a result of the intelligent and organized (planned) effort that you put out on your way to your dream. The real value of success is in the journey itself. Said even differently, success is about the character that you build as you go about accomplishing your goals and reaching for your dreams.

It is easy to see how one's decision to succeed builds character. To achieve any goal in life, you have to stay committed and persevere. In fact, successful are those who "follow through on a decision long after the excitement and emotion of the moment has passed" (Robert Cavett). Robert is another American personal development author, lawyer and a co-founder of the National Speakers Association.

There is one more observation I wish to make for the purpose of our discussion. In addition to persevering, successful people have "paid a price that is in a direct proportion to the amount of success that they have earned" (Napoleon Hill). That price is often paid in time, money, and other sacrifice. This is how the *Law of Compensation* works. As noted earlier, nothing worthwhile ever comes easy and without effort. As Zig Ziglar reminds you again:

"You were born to win but in order to win, you have to prepare, plan and expect to win"!

At last, the truth is that in order to succeed in life, you have to love what you do so you stick with it when tough times come. Whatever success means to you, know that:

Success and happiness are a decision you make!

Success and happiness are only a decision away!

And your success and happiness are only a DECISION away from YOU!

What are you waiting for?

***

The Iceberg Theory of Wealth Creation

I'd like to make a few more clarifications before we move along in our discussion. I use the terms 'wealth' and 'success' almost interchangeably, but there is a slight distinction to make. While wealth does imply financial wealth, another floating definition of wealth is everything that you have left after you have lost all of your financial possessions (money). This definition has been proposed by Roger James Hamilton, a Hong-Kong born author, educator and a renowned social entrepreneur. In his view, your wealth consists of your skills, knowledge, education, your experiences, attitudes, beliefs and habits, your social capital, ability to access other resources etc. In sum, wealth is all of your intangible assets that allow you to easily rebuild and re-create any external wealth (i.e. money) if life dealt you a curvy path. In this sense, your intangible wealth is even more precious than financial abundance. And to underscore an earlier point, the only way to build this intangible wealth successfully is by starting within. By looking within, getting honest and doing some inner foundational work.

My advice to you if I may: focus on building your 'intangibles' and you will never have to worry about the size of your bank account or the fullness of your monetary pocket. As Bruce Muzik and Roger Hamilton convincingly state, "money follows intangible wealth"! This argument is well in line with our discussion.

Build your wealth and success foundation by working with the tools and by cultivating the habits that we are about to discuss. If you do, chances are, you will narrow your current performance gap, defined as a gap between where you currently are and where you would like to be. By the time you start seeing some significant tangible results, you will have done most of your inner foundational work (alignment) that is invisible on the outside. This inner work can be compared to the two-thirds of an iceberg that can't be seen because it is submersed. And this is what I call the 'iceberg theory of wealth-creation'. Build your foundation and the rest will follow with appropriate action. Start building the intangibles so that they in turn build your tangible assets that will serve as stepping stones to your dreams and aspirations!

Your Garden of Abundance

Let's end this part of our discussion with a success analogy that further clarifies how you should be thinking about financial wealth and abundance so that you experience it in your life faster! This insightful analogy will also paint a nice visual that you can refer to freely as you start to consciously train your mind to focus on creating an abundant, happy and meaningful life for yourself and those around you.

The inspiration for this exercise came from a lecture given by Dr. Joe Vitale, another prolific self-help author also known as Mr. Fire, and who also starred in the movie the *Secret*. If you are reading this in the comfort of your home, follow me along! Close your eyes and take a few deep breaths, in and out. Now think about all aspects of wealth and success. All possible facets of success that that you can imagine or that are personally meaningful. Think about your successful, happy, financially abundant and fulfilling life and visualize it as a beautifully landscaped large royal garden. You know that you need to personally take care of this garden well for the all the bounty to manifest! This fictional bounty includes everything from financial abundance to health or anything else that you decide to intentionally plant in your garden. This could be friendships, travel, career opportunities, global exposure, commercial real-estate investments, a cottage in the mountain, a house on the lake, nice clothes, a beach house in Malibu, your own TV show etc. The sky is the limit!

Now let's carry on with our abundance analogy. When properly landscaped, cut, and attended to, your garden attracts some of the most beautiful and most exotic butterflies of different colors, sizes and hypnotizing patterns. Ranging from small to big, yellow to red, white, turquoise or green, your beautiful garden has a royal look and resembles a butterfly conservatory. Abundance flowing everywhere! Butterflies of different colors represent different forms of abundance in your life. For instance, financial abundance is represented by yellow butterflies, your friendships or social abundance is represented by orange butterflies, your health is all the greenery around, career opportunities are the abundant river flow in the back yard and so on. You see where I am going with this! Allow yourself to be playful and feel the wealth you seek to create in its many forms, shapes and colors!

Now here is where most of us go wrong with our gardening and our approach to wealth creation. Instead of attending to our garden, which consists of preparing the soil, planting, watering, weeding, plugging out anything unwanted; we spend our days trying to catch butterflies! Our efforts are often sporadic, uncoordinated and many times ineffective.

We do not realize, or maybe we forgot, that if we only took the time to attend to our garden, which is our inner reservoir and power, all of the wonderful butterflies that we are so intently after would fly into our garden freely and abundantly. If we only did the work that is required! So, I dare you! Why not try a different strategy? If you've spent most of your life trying to catch butterflies, refocus your efforts on cultivating your inner garden instead. If you attend to your garden properly, all of the abundance you seek will eventually manifest with ease. All in due time and in direct proportion to the effort put out, as the *Law of Compensation* dictates.

To start, decide what you want to have in your garden and then take all the necessary action. This means planting the right seeds and then attending to your garden on a regular basis. Look at cultivating your garden as improving yourself daily; developing and nurturing your mind, body and soul, working towards your goals etc. You will need a few tools to do the work, and that is why you may have bought this book.

One more thing to note for your benefit: while some of the information and anecdotal evidence shared throughout may seem basic to the naked untrained eye at first, the truth is, it can take years to master even a few fundamental concepts. Look at the martial arts as an example. It is not the one hundred different punches that could really hurt the opponent, but the one punch that you have practiced a thousand times that is your most powerful weapon (Kung Fu Panda). Mastering the basics or the fundamentals brings you closer to the magical. You become an expert and move with ease. On a more practical level, are you familiar with the 10,000-hour rule? Keep on reading if you are not.

***

The Evolution of Consciousness: Your Journey

If there is one book that served as my entry into the world of spirituality, I'd have to name *The Seven*

Spiritual Laws of Success by Deepak Chopra. A girlfriend of mine handed it to me about a decade ago. I did not know at the time what a profound impact it would have. Peter Guber, the former Chairman & CEO of *Sony Picture Entertainment*, compares Deepak's book to a "Virtual Reality tool-kit for the 21st-century spiritual traveler". Quite the powerful statement from an accomplished business executive.

Deepak's work, among other things, made me aware of my own spirituality, my inner power and the broader spiritual laws that govern the universe. If you are new to the field of New Thought, a spiritual movement with roots in metaphysics, I invite you to explore Deepak's work including his famous book The *Way of the Wizard: Twenty Spiritual Lessons for Creating the Life you Want.* This book sets the context for all the new information that you are about to discover in the *Spiritual MBA* handbook. One such contextual piece valuable at this point of our discussion is Deepak's proposed seven stages behind the evolution of our consciousness. These seven stages, briefly described below, are the stages that we all go through on our way to self-realization and enlightenment.

STAGES OF CONSCIOUSNESS EVOLUTION

1. **INNOCENCE**: Oneness
2. Birth of the **EGO**: birth of duality
3. Birth of the **ACHIEVER**: goals
4. Birth of the **GIVER**: ego reference still present
5. **SEEKER**: eagerness for a spiritual experience
6. **SEER**: timeless factor in the midst of a time-bound experience
7. **SPIRIT**: complete merging with consciousness

Deepak's proposed stages to awakening were adapted and reworked by others over the years. Below is another insightful adaptation discovered in an online blog (see Appendix A for a complete reference).

Stage 1: **The DRONE**: "The Sleeper, the Silent Sufferer, the Suppressor"
You are ruled by your mind and logic.
You externalize your power.

Stage 2: **The ARTIST**: "The Aware and Expressive One"
You are ruled by your heart. You are aware of your experiences and hold some power within but have not unlocked secrets to Self.

Stage 3: **The ALCHEMIST:** "The Knower of Self"
Your heart and soul are merged. As within, so without. You know that your outward experiences are a manifestation of what's within.

Stage 4: **The WIZARD**: "Master of Trinity: Mind, Body and Spirit"
You love yourself.
You understand how much you don't know.
You keep your thoughts positive.
You understand the laws of the universe and are moving through life effortlessly, encountering endless opportunities.

Here is the irony of it all! As invaluable as formal education is, it often forces us to externalize our power, which equates with the first stage of consciousness evolution. Said differently, our formal education often encourages us to look outside of ourselves for knowledge, information and external validation. Our attention is frequently called to some outside source, an outside expert, or an authority that is more credible and more knowledgeable than us. And while there are always experts that may know more than we do, can you see how this approach conditions us to feel less powerful than we really are? More often than not, formal education fails to recognize our true power, and this fact further underscores the need for a more spiritually-inspired and self-power focused development resource, such as the *Spiritual MBA*.

***

Your Spiritual Journey to Awakening

About a year ago, I was listening to an audio program recorded by Dr. Joe Vitale on the subject of spiritual awakening. I believe it was a part of the *Gold Member Hypnotic Interviews* series. While Dr. Vitale used a slightly different language to describe his four stages to awakening, you can easily identify some obvious parallels between the four stages of consciousness evolution that we had just talked about. See below and draw your own conclusions.

1. VICTIMHOOD=similar to the Drone. Your life is full of suffering and blame.
2. EMPOWERMENT=similar to the Artist. You come to your power.
3. SURRENDER=the Alchemist. You realize you are not in control.

4. AWAKENING=the Wizard. You know your true Self.

While most of us live in victimhood, the goal of this book is to start moving you toward empowerment, then surrender and final total awakening. As you can imagine, this process as can take years, especially if our egos begin to interfere in an attempt to maintain the status quo.

***

Awakening to Your True Power

"In the BEGINNING

There was neither existence nor non-existence,

All this world was un-manifest energy . . .

The One breathed, without breath, by Its own power

Nothing else was there. . ."

~Hymn of Creation, The Rig Veda~

Awakened leaders and spiritual-preneurs are in tune with their spiritual Self and allow their inner voice and their intuitive mind to guide them when needed. What you may not know is that your spiritual Self is in a constant communication with and draws on the universal intelligence that permeates the cosmos. To this point, Thomas Edison proclaimed before his death that "ideas come from space" (Claude Bristol, *The Magic of Believing*). Bristol further adds that:

> **"Men who know themselves know at once that all material things and ideas have a spiritual counterpart or basis".**

But this is not where it ends. The universal intelligence communicates with you via your inner spiritual (higher) Self and the messages are then passed down to you via your intuition. This communication is what a famous Hawaiian psychologist and a spiritual teacher Dr. Ihaleakala Hew Len calls pure inspiration. However, in order to hear it, channel it or receive it, we have to be 'clear' or 'at zero'. You will find out what 'getting clear' means in the latter part of our discussion. For now, here is an interesting fact to note about the state of Hawaii. The first syllable of the state's name, "HA", means Divinity. Discovering this Hawaiian 'HA' led me to my own 'aha' moment: let the ancient spiritual wisdom prevail!

The discovery of your spiritual nature and the 'life principle' that runs through you is what Robert Collier, another well-known author of self-help and New Thought metaphysical books, considers "the most important discovery of the modern age". He goes on to explain in his book *The Secret of the Ages* that:

"Every man can call upon this 'Life Principle' at will, and it is as much the servant of his mind as was every Aladdin's fabled 'genie-of-the-lamp. He has but to understand it and work in harmony with it to get from it anything he may need–health, happiness, riches and success".

"The ignorance of this power is the sole reason for all the failures in the world. If you would intelligently turn over to this wonderful power all your business and personal affairs in the same way that you turn over to it the mechanism of your body, no goal would be too great for you to strive for".

**

Now let's turn to you. Do you feel that there is something within you that is "urging you on to bigger things, giving you no peace, no rest, no chance to be lazy" (Collier)? Then you have awakened to this life principle and to your higher (spiritual) Self that is trying to get your attention. Did you know that your relationship with your spiritual Self is the foundation for every other relationship in your life? As within, so without.

This whisper that you keep hearing at times is your spiritual Self speaking to you through your intuition and reminding you that you can be, do and have anything and everything that you have ever set for yourself or have been always dreaming of. Do not let anything hold you back and know that it is never too late! Keep on reading to learn about specific ways to unlock the powers of this personal genie of yours.

***

The Spiritual-MBA Way or Spiritual Preneurship

"Spirituality is the knowingness that we are all connected to each other and to something much larger than ourselves".

~Suzanne West, the *Huffington Post*~

The question remains: How does one build a happy, fulfilling and prosperous life the spiritual way and how do we know that we have arrived? According to Deepak Chopra, we have achieved true success when…

"we begin to experience our life as the MIRACULOUS expression of Divinity – then we will

know the true meaning of success! True success is the unfolding of the Divinity within us".

~The Seven Spiritual Laws of Success~

My personal experiences and observations led me to one fundamental belief: we can go through life with more joy, ease and fulfillment, we can give more and get more out of life, if we upgrade our day-to-day habits, raise our standards and live in line with the principles of what I call **Spiritual-Preneurship**: a spiritually-inspired self-leadership. To Deepak's definition of success above, spiritual-preneurs do experience these moments of miraculous and it is time for you to do the same, if you feel so inclined! To set a baseline for our discussion, I have prepared a list of attributes and actions that embody the essence of this spiritually-inspired and entrepreneurial self-leadership framework.

Awareness and Empowerment. Understanding of HIGHER Laws and Higher Self. Clear Vision of Self and the Future. Optimistic ANTICIPATION. Enthusiasm. Committed Passionate Effort. Inspired Massive Action. Focus and CONCENTRATION. Expansive IMAGINATION. Pleasing Personality. Love. Joy. Willingness to Learn. Willingness to Change.

Karmic GIVING. Useful Service. Unparalleled FAITH. Remarkable Initiative & Self-Control. SMART Goals and HYPNOTIC Intentions.

Spiritually-inspired Success HABITS. Spiritual Leadership TOOLKIT. Strong Positive Self-Image & CONFIDENCE. Organized Effort. FOCUSED Plan. Habit of Saving. DREAM-BUILDING. Playful Visualization. SUCCESS Scripting. VISUALIZED Meditation. INTUITIVE Mind. Inner Power. ACCURATE Thought. Mind Sync. Tolerance. The Golden Rule etc.

Spiritual-preneurship sets out a new paradigm: a new spiritually-rooted approach to leading yourself on your path to self-realization and living in line with the universal laws. Spiritual-preneurship is a code of conduct and a pre-requisite step to living an abundant, healthy, happy, and fulfilling life that lasts, while making a positive contribution to the world.

A quick administrative note: for the remainder of the book, the terms 'spiritual-MBA', enlightened entrepreneur, awakened leader and spiritual-preneur are used interchangeably. Let's have a quick glance at the concept of spiritual-preneurship.

As a SPIRITUAL-PRENEUR...

You are an AWAKENED leader who is aware of self and others and sees himself or herself as a spiritual being first. The physical (human) experience is second. You understand the illusion of separation and are aware that at some level, you are one with the Universe. You aware of your true powers and your untapped potential and allow yourself to be guided by your intuitive Self.

You understand and work in harmony with the HIGHER LAWS that govern the universe. You know that these laws work as precisely as the *Law of Gravity*. Other examples of such laws are the more frequently referenced *Law of Attraction*, or the *Law of Cause and Effect*, also known as the *Law of Karma*.

You have developed and keep nurturing a positive and AFFIRMATIVE mindset. You know that your mindset is the key to living a happy and abundant life, as it sets the tone for how you approach and respond to everyone and everything that goes on in your day, week, month, year or a lifetime. An affirmative mindset empowers you and helps you build other positive success habits. When it comes to your desires and dreams, you view them as already fulfilled. In other words, you act and feel as if you already have that, which you have intended to get.

You focus on building your INNER value first. You know that your external wealth is an exact reflection of what's on the inside. You know that by building yourself from within, you manifest and experience in the physical world correspondingly. You know that success is about whom you become as a result of the journey you take and are grateful for all the learning opportunities that further strengthened your already sound character.

You are love-based and INTUITIVE, as opposed to being only fact-based, rational, linear and logical. You are aware of the limitations of linear thinking and the dangers of overthinking. You love yourself (self-love), love your life and send love to everything you seek to manifest, create and experience. You send love to everyone that you interact with and wish abundance, health and happiness to all. You know that love is the highest vibrating emotion and carries the greatest creative power. You also know that LOVE neutralizes the ego.

You are grateful and APPRECIATIVE. You work within an INTEGRATIVE & collaborative rather than a competitive spirit. You know that competition is based on the principle of scarcity, a key assumption in economics. Wikipedia defines scarcity as "the gap between a limited or scarce resource and theoretically limitless wants", also known as the supply-demand gap. As a spiritual-preneur, you do not hold scarcity in your vocabulary or mental mindset. You are focused on creating innovative sustainable outcomes by being inclusive and delivering lasting value, even if at the expense of short-term profits. You live to render useful service and make a positive impact on your families, communities, countries, depending on your sphere of influence.

You understand that your mind is a large broadcasting station of ideas. You therefore realize the importance of maintaining a high vibrational FREQUENCY at all times. You focus on activities that make you feel good and are filled with appreciation, gratitude and other positive emotions. You eradicated the negative from your verbal and mental vocabulary.

You know that time is an illusion. You know that the true nature of time is not what and how your mind perceives it to be. In fact, the only moment that truly matters is now. You are aware of the power of NOW and welcome, appreciate and seize each present moment. You take IMMEDIATE action that is inspired by the Higher power. You understand that action is rewarded and unlocks the *Law of Attraction*.

You are committed to continuous learning & SELF-DEVELOPMENT. You strive to better yourself every day. You remain 'teachable' past your formal education because you know that not learning and growing leads to stagnation. Continuous personal development has become your success habit.

You embrace CHANGE and understand the power of committed and passionate focus when it comes to implementing and sustaining any change initiatives. You follow through on your change efforts and respect and deliver on all agreements that you make to yourself and/or others.

You realize that HAPPINESS comes from within and it is about BEING and not about doing. You allow yourself to just BE and spend some time in stillness and silence as frequently as possible.

When it comes to the level of self-leadership mastery, you are at the level of unconscious COMPETENCE or an autopilot! You have internalized powerful success-building tactics and principles and they have become an integral part of your subconscious programming and guide our external behavior. This is a crucial step, as it anchors and solidifies your newly developed success habits. As Zig Ziglar remarks:

"If you are going to do anything well, you must move it from the conscious to the subconscious mind"!

**

THE 10,000-HOUR RULE

Now let's do a creative math exercise to get your whole-brain thinking involved.

Have you ever heard of Malcolm Gladwell's **10,000-hour rule**? According to this Canadian journalist, author and public speaker most known for his best-sellers *Blink: The Power of Thinking Without Thinking* and *Outliers: The Story of Success*, it takes about 10,000 hours of focused activity to become an expert in any field. If you have your phone calculators ready, you can follow the math with me. Take 10,000 hours and divide by 24 (hours). In line with Malcolm's rule, it would take you 416.66666666 days or just over a year to develop an area of expertise, while practicing 24 hours a day, seven days a week. Impossible! If you decided to dedicate a conservative 2 hours a day to your practice, you would achieve mastery in 5,000 days, which equals to approximately 166 months or 13.8 years. At a typical 8-hour working day, one reaches the level of mastery at 1,250 days, which equals to approximately 41.6 months or 3.4 years.

The purpose of this exercise was to give you a point of reference. Over the past six years, I have dedicated on average 3 hours a day to personal and professional development, including the study of success and various success principles at large. That makes it over 6,000 hours of focused activity.

***

New Thought and the Mind Stuff

I know that you want more out of life! I also know that you are looking for new, more effective and perhaps more spiritual way to get there. I know it because you bought this book and got to this point. Congratulations! You are already stand out! You are in the top 25% reading percentile as 75% of Americans do not read on a regular basis. On this note, did you know that the most effective way to read is in 20-minute increments? That is when your mind is most receptive to new information. After about 20 minutes, our focus decreases as our mind starts to wonder to our to-do lists or any other distractions. When this happens, you are best to change up the activity, as your reading will not be as effective. Take a stretch break or do a breathing meditation exercise and then resume your reading. And now back to our chapter headline. New Thought and the mind stuff.

Serendipity. A 2001 romantic comedy starring Kate Beckinsale and John Cusack. Its dictionary definition:

"Serendipity: the concurrence and development of events by chance in a happy and beneficial way".

It was a fortunate stroke of serendipity that put Rhonda Byrne's book *the Secret* into my hands that day! A kind gesture from a completely unexpected new friendship. Thank you, Amanda! The awakening phase of my spiritual journey could not have been triggered in any more serendipitous way, I thought to myself! I met a random friend on a random evening that by chance handed me a book that made a spiritual splash, created an opening and made me curious to know more! If you are familiar with Rhonda's book or the movie, your mind is well neutralized for the information I am about to present next.

In fact, the information and many of the principles revealed in this book pertain to the field of New (Higher) Thought, a spiritual movement with beliefs rooted in metaphysics. This movement developed in the United States in the 19th century and is considered by many to have been derived from the unpublished writings of Phineas Quimby, a spiritual teacher and an inventor. Modern-day adherents of this field share some core beliefs. They believe that Infinite Intelligence is universal, and we are spiritual beings first. "Spirit is the totality of all real things and our mental states and images manifest into physical reality" (Wikipedia).

***

The Untold Story of the Brain: Biology 101

What do you remember from your high-school biology class about the brain? If you paid attention, you may recall that your brain is composed of grey and white matter and you most likely equate it with your reasoning mind. What you may not know is that there are over 80 billion nerve cells (neurons) in your cerebral cortex and over 100 billion neuro-pathways, making a total of 100 trillion connections (Wikipedia).

If you are interested in proper nutrition, you may know that among top brain boosters are fatty acids (fish), almonds, apples, asparagus, avocados, bananas, beans, bell peppers, beets, broccoli and blueberries. You may have heard the term left-brain and right-brain thinking, but this is where your brain-knowledge most likely stops, unless you are a neuro-surgeon or another brain specialist. I was not an exception. It was to my surprise that afternoon as my eyes paused on the following statement written by Napoleon Hill. This claim about our subconscious mind is also upheld by the scientific community.

"It is INCONCEIVABLE that such a network of intricate machinery should be in existence for the sole purpose of carrying on the physical functions incidental to growth and maintenance of the physical body".

The subconscious mind is the sending station of the brain, through which vibrations of thought are broadcast. The creative imagination is the "receiving set" through which the vibrations of thought are picked up from the ether".

What I was reading surprised me. Comparing brain to a giant broadcasting station seemed like such a simple and effective analogy, yet, none of my formal teachers ever articulated a similar thought. While this whole notion of my brain acting as a broadcasting station and my ability to create through my thoughts seemed rather strange to me at first, my inner voice told me to remain open and experiment a bit.

And experiment I did! I began to consciously view my brain as a giant satellite dish that sends and receives messages in the form of various frequencies. I started to view it as a large and powerful broadcasting stations of my dreams and goals. What I want you to remember from this discussion is that your thoughts are pure energy and each thought, and its corresponding emotional state has an inherent energetic frequency. This frequency acts as a 'code' so to speak that communicates the nature of your thoughts and emotions to the outside world. While your thought vibrations are invisible to the naked eye, every thought and emotion that originates within you is being broadcasted into the ether in the form of a frequency. Whether your outgoing frequency is serving you or holding you back depends on the nature of your thoughts and emotions, with love vs. anger being the most obvious example of a vibrational contrast. For a detailed list of various emotional states and their corresponding energetic frequencies, please refer to the *Map of Consciousness* in Appendix F.

For your convenience, below is a list of some of the most commonly encountered emotions and their corresponding frequencies. It goes without saying that the higher the vibrational frequency of the underlying outgoing message (thought or emotion), the more positive your subsequent real-life experience. The numerical information below has been adapted from a *Map of Consciousness* prepared by David R. Hawkins (see Appendix A). The numbers attached represent the energetic frequency associated with a particular emotion. If you are familiar with the concept of a glycemic index (GI) in nutrition, energetic frequency works just the same, but in reverse. The lower the GI, the healthier the food. When it comes to your thoughts and emotions, the low-vibrating thoughts and emotions need to be shown the door! Here is a general 'rule of thumb': the higher your overall energetic frequency, the more joyful, rewarding and effortless your life experience.

JOY: 540

LOVE: 500

FORGIVENESS: 350

OPTIMISM: 310
ANGER & HATE: 150
ANXIETY & FEAR: 100
BLAME & GUILT: 30
SHAME: 20

As noted earlier, every thought and emotion that originates within your mind is released to the ether. The energetic data of your message keeps floating in the ether until it is picked up by other similar frequencies. This is precisely the *Law of Attraction* at work! For the very same reason, angry people tend to attract other angry people and similar circumstances that make them even more angry, while happy people magnetize more happiness, love and peace. It really could not be any simpler; yet we often vainly work against this universal principle. And for those not familiar with the word 'ether' also called the 'quintessence', it is "the material that fills the region of the universe above the terrestrial zone, according to ancient and medieval science" (Wikipedia).

Here is a simple and insightful exercise that you can do now or at your own leisure! It is also a good way to reinforce the concept of energetic frequency that we are discussing. Go to Appendix F and study the *Map of*

Consciousness closely to calculate an estimate of your average daily vibrational frequency. Here is an external benchmark to guide your assessment. Winners keep at least 85% of their daily thoughts and emotions positive, at a high 500+. Can you say the same about yourself? Luckily, you are not required to do any calculations to know where you stand energetically. You have a much more predictable and already built-in barometer for assessing your outgoing energetic frequency. Stay tuned to find out what that is! Do you aspire to be an Ivy League material? Then join other spiritual-preneurs who have mastered to keep their energetic 'GMAT score' at a high 500 plus.

***

LIKE likes LIKE

Let's look at another example of how your overall vibration determines what you experience on a day-to-day basis. Let's suppose you bought a table for eight at a local fundraiser. Because of your sizeable contribution, you end up winning the evening's draw and walk away with a nice gift. You give even this bonus gift away to your friend, as she desperately needs it. It is a trip for two in the Caribbean that she has been dreaming about but cannot afford at the moment. As the universe would have it, three months later, you sign a very lucrative contract that was referred to you by a new business contact that you met at that charity event! Have you ever experienced a similar scenario? If you did, you already know that the universe works in mysterious ways and often surprises us, if we bother to act in alignment with its natural laws! When you vibrate love, happiness, abundance and joy, the universe delivers more of the same. In this case, you attracted a positive circumstance - a new lucrative client - that matched the vibrational frequency of your generosity and your thoughts of abundance. This is what put you in a vibrational alignment with the universal flow to begin with!

I advise you to digest this information carefully and realize that these laws work just the same in the negative. It is therefore paramount that you learn how to control your behavioral and emotional responses to situations, people and events! You get what you send out and there is no sense in losing your cool over your coffee not being served hot enough at a local Starbucks, for instance. Low-vibrating emotions and reactions do nothing, but keep you stuck in a low-vibrating cycle, and this only puts a spoke in your wheel of success.

Instead, you should be riding the 'success momentum' that we will talk about shortly.

To bring this point home, we all know people who constantly complain about this or that, but who never fully take responsibility for their life's circumstance. Another good example are folks who live with a million regrets and excuses and unknowingly keep themselves in the low-20 frequency. By becoming more self-aware, you can navigate yourself out of the destructive negative waters and make more significant leaps of forward momentum in both your personal and professional lives.

***

The Seven Most Extreme Emotions

This is probably the shortest segment of this book, but one that cannot be omitted. Throughout my entrepreneurial career and my life at large, I have seen many good opportunities and relationships wasted due to strong egos and some of the negative emotions listed here. In line with our discussion on vibrational frequencies, I give you a list of the seven most negative, most damaging and lowest vibrating emotions that will surely sabotage or at least stall any of your attempts at building a happy and successful life for yourself. The list was compiled by Napoleon Hill following decades of his committed study of success and achievement. In no particular order are:

The emotion of **FEAR**
The emotion of JEALOUSY
The emotion of **HATRED**
The emotion of REVENGE
The emotion of **GREED**
The emotion of SUPERSTITION
The emotion of **ANGER**

Here is another secret! Positive and negative emotions cannot occupy your mind at the same time! What is the practical implication? As an aspiring spiritual-preneur, you need to eradicate all negative emotions from your repertoire and replace them by empowering, high-vibrating positive emotions that have a positive transformational effect on your life and your day-to-day actions and behaviors. I now give you the seven most POSITIVE emotions, as proposed by Napoleon Hill. In no particular order:

The emotion of DESIRE
The emotion of **FAITH**

The emotion of ENTHUSIASM

The emotion of **LOVE**

The emotion of ROMANCE

The emotion of **HOPE**

The emotion of XXX

I know you are wondering, but I am not at liberty to disclose the last positive element. You will have to get a copy of Napoleon's book to complete the list or you can always connect with me. Before we proceed, I encourage you to conduct an honest self-assessment against these two lists and see what negative emotions you may still be an energetic slave to. Many of us have an ongoing fight with the emotions of fear, anger or jealousy. Spiritual-preneurs, on the other hand, feel as enthusiastic about successes of others, as they do about their own! This idea is a key characteristic of the proposed spiritual-preneurship and is also discussed in Joe Vitale's book titled *The Awakened Millionaire: A Manifesto for the Spiritual Wealth Movement.*

***

The Whole-Brain Genius

Let's carry on with our discussion about the brain and its main and most commonly known function: the thinking process. Most traditional educational institutions and Ivy League schools encourage and reward logical, analytical, and objective thinking that originates in the left side of your brain. As you may know, the left-side of your brain is pragmatic, more mathematical and scientific. Nonetheless, to live a successful and fulfilling well-rounded life, you also have to tap into the right side of your brain. The right side is more emotional, intuitive, subjective, more spontaneous and more connected to the spiritual dimension of your being. By leveraging and tapping into your right-brain, you are also connecting to the universal flow of energy and the universal intelligence.

Whole-brain thinking is of tremendous value and as science has proven, it has the potential of taking us to a genius level (*Psychology Today*). In case you did not know, Einstein was a whole-brain thinker and so is Sir Richard Branson! To our detriment, our society over-emphasizes logical thinking and often associates the right-brain intuitive thinking with ultra-creative types such as artists, musicians, movie directors etc.

The importance of tapping into both sides of our brain should not be underestimated. In fact, our mind (brain) is 50% visual and it is the right side of the brain that processes any visual and creative imagery, including intuitive messages. To this point, an article published in a *Harvard Business Review* concluded that about 80% of accomplished entrepreneurs attributed their successes to relying on their intuition (McLaughlin). We will circle back to this point shortly. But now...

***

Let's Get Meta-Physical

Metaphysics "is the branch of philosophy that studies the essence of a thing. This includes questions of being, becoming, existence, and reality" (Wikipedia).

You know from our previous discussion that your brain sends and receives frequencies all day long, whether awake or sleeping. Let's push this thought one step further. Your thinking and emotional patterns shape and define your energy field, which in turn shapes your overall life experience. Said differently, your physiology changes depending on your energy field that is shaped by what you are thinking and feeling. Therefore, your thoughts and emotions co-create your reality! Let's look at how this plays out in an everyday scenario.

IMAGINE that you just had a fight with your friend or a significant other and they made you really angry! You feel this anger in every cell of your body, but deep down, you feel partly guilty for starting the fight by being argumentative. At least you are aware enough, you think to yourself. Here is the y point.

If you lack sufficient self-control and fail to keep a tight lid on your emotional responses to situations, you will lose control over what you experience in your day-to-day situations. If nothing changes, you will lose control over your aggregate life experience or your *Incredible Life* movie! Not a pleasant thought, is it? If you allow negative thoughts and emotions drag you down and pollute your energetic field, your life circumstance will reflect this low vibrational frequency. The universe will respond to you in kind, by trading anger for anger, one fight for even a bigger one. In other words, it will keep bringing you circumstances, people and events that line up with your overall frequency, unless you become aware and make a conscious vibrational shift. Bottom line: put your creative power to a good use and do not waste it on emotions like anger, fear or jealousy. If someone lives the life of your dreams, learn from them and consider them your role-model. Celebrate their successes and more reasons for you to celebrate will be given to you.

***

Secrets About Your Subconscious

As you know by now, the mental power that governs the functioning of your physical body is only a small fraction of all the power that is available to you. Other than thinking, learning, reasoning, the most important function of your conscious mind is to "focus your thoughts on the things you want, and to shut off the door on every suggestion of fear or worry or disease" (Robert Collier). But your logical mind alone cannot manifest your desires.

As far as your subconscious mind goes, we tend to have a limited view of its functions and often reference it in conversations about bad dreams and nightmares. Not too often do we create an explicit link between the creative power of our subconscious, our business results, relationships, life goals and/or degree of happiness. Due to insufficient education on this topic, we underestimate the creative power of our precious internal machinery: our subconscious mind. And even if we awaken to this power, we often lack the right tools to properly harness its creative potential.

So what else is there to know about your subconscious? To start, your subconscious is a distinct entity from your conscious mind and it permeates your entire body. As Robert Collier describes it:

"Your subconscious is beyond space and time it embodies the feeling and wisdom of the past, the awareness and knowledge of the present, and the thought and vision of the future"!

What this means is that you have within you the power to be, do and have anything and everything that your mind can conceive of and determines to bring into a physical existence. Your subconscious is of limitless power and this is where your true creative self-power resides. It pays to have a clearly understanding of its main functions and abilities. In a way, your subconscious mind is your magic wand! Below is a more detailed description of its various functions and attributes as outlined by Robert Collier.

The SUBCONSCIOUS mind:

1. Controls all involuntary functions; all voluntary functions are controlled by your conscious mind.

2. Can see without the use of physical eyes. It sees things that "no regular sight can behold".
3. Has the power to communicate with the unspoken world.
4. Can read thoughts of others.
5. Perceives by intuition.
6. Receives intelligence and transmits it to people at distance.

**

Other experts have elaborated on the functions of our subconscious. Dr. Winbigler published an article in *Practical Psychology and Sex Life*, where he claims that the subconscious:

1) Carries out the work of assimilation while we sleep.
2) Reveals to us things that the conscious mind has no conception of until they occur.
3) It approves and disapproves of a code of conduct and conversations.
4) It carries out all the best things, which are given to it, provided that the conscious mind does not intercept and change the course of its manifestation.

Your subconscious mind is in turn connected to the universal intelligence that houses all knowledge and wisdom and that your subconscious draws on when working out solutions to assigned problems or when orchestrating the manifestation of your desires. As Collier remarks to this point:

"There is within you–within everyone–this mighty resistless force with which you can perform undertakings that will dazzle your reason, stagger your imagination. There constantly resides within you a mind that is all-wise, all-powerful, a mind that is entirely apart from the mind that you consciously use on your everyday affairs".

***

Brain Integrity

Have you ever heard of 'brain integrity'? It's a concept I caught on the radio one afternoon and the catchy phrase got me curious. Thanks to Google, I had all the necessary information at my fingertips within seconds. Ah, the beauty of living in the digital age!

What brain integrity does is this: it takes what we verbally say or think and causes everything in us to physically manifest these thoughts and words. This goes back to our earlier discussion about how your thoughts, words and emotions shape your energetic field. Or, in the great words of Buddha:

"All that we are is the result of what we have thought".

Thoughts and words become things. Therefore, think differently today to witness a new life tomorrow! Monitor your feelings and watch your words because you are creating every minute, whether you are conscious of it, or not. Change your mental diet and eliminate all negative input to see changes in your physical world. And now time for some more trivia. Did you know that the phrase 'ABRACADABRA', that we associate with wizards and witches from fairy-tales, actually means "YOU CREATE AS YOU SPEAK" in Hebrew? If there is one key point in this section to take away, it is this: your words, thoughts and dominant emotional states create your daily reality.

Here is an interesting story. My guess is, you may have experienced a similar situation. It is Wednesday morning and you have a staff meeting. You remember, as you are walking to the boardroom, that you forgot to draft up that sales report. You get a bit worried because it is one week overdue, and your boss is not in a very good mood. You say to yourself: "I hope she doesn't call upon me this morning". What happens at the meeting? You are asked to present the very report that you forgot to prepare.

I have two points to emphasize. First, it was your thoughts (step 1) and the power of your spoken word (step 2) that partly put you in this situation. Your subtle fear of being called upon intensified any negative thoughts. While we often view these situations in reference to Murphy's law, we are the ones who create the very outcomes we experience, even if we are not aware. Visualize only positive circumstances, events and encounters if that is what you wish to bring into your physical experience. Of course, you also have to be internally aligned, which is an important topic that we will come back to later.

Let's now proceed with a more positive example of how brain integrity shows up in everyday life. This is a personal anecdote and another testament to the effectiveness of this information. About 5 years ago, my partner and I took a cruise in the Caribbean. After the cabin check-in, I walked into the spa to participate in a contest because I was about to win! That was my expectation the minute I set my foot on that ship. To bump up my chances of winning, I kept visualizing my name being drawn from the giant wheel filled with slips. And there it was! I ended winning the first prize! I even have a photo from the contest as tangible proof.

This story exemplifies many key manifestation points. It was my attitude, mindset and focus on wining, coupled with an unparalleled belief and a feeling of having already won that resulted in me winning a nice spa package, compliments of the Royal Caribbean! While I was still in the testing stage of my newfound wealth creation principles, I was quite impressed with the result that day, I must add. Was it a coincidence? No one will ever know but I do not personally think so. This and many other similar eye-opening experiences further reinforced my belief and commitment to my new field of study.

One of my goals in this book is to remind you that you have a very precious asset at your creative disposal. I am here to remind that your mind is your biggest asset and how you use it is completely up to you! In line with the concept of brain integrity, I suggest you don't give it away too freely on useless bickering and arguments. Rather, use it to lift yourself to incredible heights of success, making a positive difference on those around you and the world at large. Remember Zig Ziglar's words?

"You were designed for accomplishment, engineered for success and endowed with the seeds of greatness"!

***

The Not-so-Strange Secret

The very idea that thoughts become things and we become our thoughts is captured in a 1957 motivational audio recording that became a true classic. It is called the *Strangest Secret* by Earl Nightingale. Please see Appendix A for a link to this audio or look it up on YouTube.

Even this recording has a unique story. "It sold over a million copies and received the first *Gold Record* for the spoken word, which helped launch the fields of business motivation and audio publishing" (Wikipedia). If you have never heard the *Strangest Secret* or listened to any of Earl's Nightingale's recordings, you can add them to your list of self-development resources. The *Strangest Secret* directs your attention to a few fundamental truths that we often conveniently disregard as we go about our life and are then surprised with the consequences that we experience. What is this strangest secret, you ask? It is this simple, yet truthful observation that

"YOU BECOME WHAT YOU THINK ABOUT"!

**

Said differently, it is the sum of your thoughts that largely determines the kind of life that you live. Think negatively, complain, judge and criticize and your life will throw at you more of the same. Think positive thoughts, be grateful, expect everything to work out, while taking the necessary action, and your overall life experience will be significantly more pleasant and rewarding. It seems rather simple, but this is how the universe works. And yes, Earl Nightingale's secret is essentially the *Law of Attraction* at work.

Are you looking for more proof? Think of an optimist and a pessimist that you know. Whose life would you rather live? The 2017 movie *Father Figures* starring Owen Wilson and Ed Helms is a suitable relevant illustration. It portrays a story of two diametrically opposed twin-brothers. An eccentric, and overly optimistic Kyle with a pleasing personality, who capitalized on a business invention and is living the life in LA (Owen Wilson). On the other end of the spectrum is his grumpy twin brother Peter, who lives in victimhood and blames just about everyone and everything for his miserable existence. Do you see how they both co-created their realities? As life would have it, Kyle and Peter are forced by an external circumstance to take a trip together in order to find their biological father. Over the course of their journey, they both learn from each other and Peter goes through a significant turning point or a moment of awakening. He realizes that he never really thought about what it is that he wanted out of life. Instead, he kept making choices that kept everyone else, but himself happy. Is this resonating at some level? Be grateful if it is! Self-awareness is the first step to any breakthroughs or transformation.

Desire is the First Law of Gain

If you had a magic wand in your hands, what would you wish for? More money, better health, bigger house, more time, love, travel, freedom? Whatever it is, identifying and defining what you want is your starting point. The second step entails hypnotizing your goal in your mind so that it becomes magnetic and draws the right circumstances and people to you. So here is the next nugget of wisdom.

"Whatever you desire wholeheartedly - with the singleness of purpose - you can have! But […] you've got to know what you want before you stand much chance of getting it. You have an unfailing "Messenger to Garcia" in that Genie-of-Your-Mind- but YOU have to formulate the message".

~Robert Collier, *The Secret of the Ages*~

Unfortunately, if you are like the majority, you can probably name faster that which you do not want; you may struggle giving a detailed description of the life of your dreams or are lacking a clear vision of such life all together. And this is another debilitating paradox to watch out for! As Robert Collier further observes, most people are so "taken up with the struggle that they have forgotten–if they ever knew–what it is that they are struggling for". To this point, he adds:

"Aladdin would have stood a poor chance of getting anything from his Genie, if he had not clearly seen in his mind the things that he wanted the Genie to get".

**

Wherever you are at this point in time, that is where you start! It is absolutely crucial that you only give your undivided focus and attention to that which you seek to experience in your life. This could be anything from tangible things and assets, to experiences, skills, relationships, the choice is yours. But, before you can focus on it, you have to identify and define your dreams, goals, the ultimate outcomes you seek. You have to clearly know and see in your mind what it is that you are after, so that you can set powerful intentions and engage all of your senses in the creative process. In line with the *Law of Intention and Desire*, your "attention energizes and your intentions shape and transform the quantum field" (Chopra). We will discuss goals and intentions in more detail shortly. For now, remember that setting specific goals activates the left side of your brain.

Let's now play a quick game for the sake of illustration. If you are reading this at home, take a blank piece of paper or use your smart phone notes. Here comes your challenge.

You SUDDENLY have access to **$11,000,000**. You have 33 minutes to spend it or you lose it all. Think about it well and write down how you would spend this money. You need at least 5 items on your list. Here is the real test: if this scenario really occurred right now, would you be able to spend $11,000,000 in 33 minutes, on the spot? And how do you think it would make you feel?

If you breezed through the challenge, let's increase the level of difficulty. How about spending, or at least allocating, $44,000,000 = $44 Million dollars? What about $444,000,000 = $444 Million? Clearly, you would need a bit more time to spend almost a half a billion. You may also see that spending even $44 Million is not as easy and requires a well thought out plan. And if even this exercise was a piece of cake, then you are in the top percentile.

On the other hand, if spending even $11 Million was a problem for you, why would the universe entrust you with that amount or more? Think about it! Dollars come to those who know what to do with it and have a detailed plan for its use.

***

This or Something Better

While knowing what you want is key, it is equally essential to embed some flexibility to your expectations around the final outcome. There are various ways that your desire or goal could end up manifesting, so give yourself and the universe some room to maneuver.

Imagine that you are planning another vacation. Work has been crazy, it is freezing outside, and you need to get away! You normally take a cruise but this time, you want to go somewhere new. You set the intention and remain open to the possibilities. A week later, you are out with friends and are introduced to a new girlfriend who just moved to town. You hit it off! A month later, she invites you to spend a week at her parents' place in Palm Springs, California. True story! Synchronicity or serendipity? Perhaps both. The key was to remain open about the end result (i.e. vacation destination), while expecting only the best outcome! The vacation was amazing, and we created many fond memories!

To signal to the universe that you are flexible, I am about to give you two easy-to-remember phrases that act as your manifestation levers, so to speak. These statements are powerful as they communicate flexibility around the end result, releasing limiting expectations and allowing for the unfoldment of endless possibilities. These phrases also signal that you trust the universe in assisting you with the fulfillment of your desires. The added bonus of remaining flexible is that the universe often surprises you with something even better than you may have initially conceived of!

These two magic sentences, that you attach to the formulation of your goals and intentions, are…

"This, or something better"!

"What's best for all involved or what is in the highest good for all involved"!

Let me provide one more example: let's suppose you want to sell a new designer fashion line in physical retail stores across the USA. You have a specific retail chain in mind. You set your intention, write it down and end with one of the statements above. It turns out that a new online channel presented itself unexpectedly and you decide to pursue it. At the end, this distribution channel is generating so much business that you don't even need to consider selling through physical retail stores anymore. I invite you to start adding these two phrases to your goals and intentions and let the universe do its magic along your committed efforts! This brings me to our next topic.

Harnessing the Power: Focus & Concentration

September 11, 2018. *The Standard*. Today's headline reads:

PASSIONATE COMMITTED FOCUS CREATES SUCCESS!

Let me ask you the following. Do you know exactly what it is that you are aiming for in life? Do you have a clear vision for yourself, your business, family, community or your city? Is this vision yours or somebody else's? You know that your starting point is identifying and thoroughly describing exactly what you want. And a vague idea or a mere wish will not cut it. You have to clearly articulate what Napoleon Hill calls your "singleness or definiteness of purpose" or your "definite chief aim". I encourage you to think about these questions seriously, as many of us find ourselves pursuing unsatisfying paths that we are afraid to leave. If your life experience is no longer fulfilling, your current focus may be out of alignment with your life's mission. In this case, you may need to re-calibrate.

Part of your daily focus work entails the management of your thoughts or what I call a regular 'thought-maintenance' work. As you now know, we all have the occasional negative thought roam in our mind, a rather destructive thought that needs to be taken out. Your primary goal is to keep your thoughts fixed and focused on the successful accomplishment of your dreams, goals and intentions. Spiritual-preneurs know that committed focus energizes, intensifies and magnifies their thoughts of success and corresponding actions. Passionate focus intensifies the creative power of your ideas and raises your energetic frequency. The more you focus on an idea, the stronger your vibration, and the faster its manifestation. Of course, your focus has to be accompanied by an unparalleled belief.

I admit, it is sometimes easy to get distracted in this fast-paced world by yet another mobile device, social medial or an app demanding your instant attention. Spiritual-preneurs know to identify their key priorities clearly and on a regular basis and focus on them systematically, because focus creates success. Positive focused thought leads to positive outcomes. As Rhonda Byrne puts it:

"Nothing can come into your experience unless you summon it through persistent thought".

Here is an insightful analogy so that you fully grasp the power of committed focus. It is also an essential success habit. Imagine a scorching hot day! The temperature hitting almost 90 degrees. You forgot your mom's magnifying glass on the wooden table on the patio. Similar to your focus, the magnifying glass keeps intensifying the sun rays hitting it. If left unattended, you may be walking into a fire situation. On a similar note, your focus energizes and has the potential to bring about fire, both physical and metaphorical. That is how powerful its creative energy and its ability to propel you forward. That internal fire, if properly harnessed, leads to committed effort, aggressive action, progress, and success! So essential is concentration to the pursuit of happiness and achievement that Napoleon Hill named it one of his 16 key principles of success. He goes on to explain:

"Nothing was ever created by a human being which was not first created in the imagination, through desire, and then translated into reality through concentration".

**

Concentration is the ability to think as you wish to think. It is "the ability to control your thoughts and direct them to a definite end, and the ability to organize your knowledge into a plan of action that is sound and workable" (Hill). Obviously, this "focused work" cannot be happening in your mind alone. To get results, you need to follow with consistent action, as noted above. I leave you with one more inspirational quote on the subject of personal commitment. It is a personal favorite and I hope that it lights your own internal fire! The quote is by Kelly M. Beard, a spiritual astrologer.

"At the time of commitment, the Universe conspires to assist you"!

In response to your commitment and focused effort, the universe almost re-arranges itself to send you the perfect set of circumstances, giving a metaphorical helping hand in manifesting your desires. Understand and work this magic! The more passionate committed action you take, the more universal alignment and synchronicity you will experience. I also invite you to check out Kelly's energy forecasts posted on a Spirit library website weekly (Appendix A). Kelly's forecasts are concise, insightful and quite accurate.

For the sake of full disclosure, I regularly follow one more astrologer that came recommended through a dear friend. Susan Miller is a New Yorker who started her career in business, but her expertise in astrology was sought out even by the White House. She has millions of followers globally and can be found at www.astrologyzone.com. Why astrology? I pay attention to key planetary movements and their respective influences on those aspects of our lives that these planets govern. For instance, the planet Mercury rules the field of communications. Put simply, astrology for me is just another data point. It is also an ancient science that sheds a unique light on the energies of the broader context (the universe) that we all play our game of life within. My view is: the more information I have, the more effective my decision-making and the more satisfying the final outcomes. Are you ready to hear another secret?

THE 68-SECOND MAGIC!

The high-tech and digital age we live in has facilitated many scientific breakthroughs and discoveries. Two such discoveries are worth mentioning when it comes to the subject of focus.

Scientists have uncovered that long-term committed focus alters brain chemistry. Specifically, both your grey and white matter grow when you keep focused on a goal long-enough. The second discovery is pure magic if you are ready to see it. The scientific community now knows that it takes exactly **68** seconds of focused thinking for your energy field to start re-arranging itself so that your thought starts to manifest itself into a physical form. Seems hard to believe? Perhaps it will be more believable when you learn that a block of 17 seconds of concentrated and committed focus is believed to "generate an expansion energy equivalent to 2,000 action-hours" (Abraham Hicks). Bottom line: your focused thoughts are very powerful.

Please allow me to introduce a very useful formula that you can combine with the above scientific finding and use to your absolute advantage! I call it a Manifestation Mantra. It was scripted by Napoleon Hill to help you focus your mind on a particular goal or your 'chief aim' that you had identified for yourself. It takes about 68 seconds to write out or say out-loud, just the right amount of time for your thoughts to start getting a foothold in their physical manifestations. I sincerely hope that you take advantage and use it constructively. Select a goal that is dear to you and rewrite this 'mantra' on an index card with a blue pen. Why blue? I'll tell you soon!

Read this mantra with an absolute faith aloud daily, just before you get up in the morning and before you go to bed at night. After you write it down, I suggest going one step further and memorizing it. Training your memory this way is as beneficial to your brain-health as engaging in crossword puzzles! And if it has been a while since you have been in school, give your brain some exercise and memorize this powerful poem.

**

MANIFESTATION MANTRA

For the purpose of the exercise, let's use '*top earning account executive*' as a desired outcome. You can substitute any goal of your choice, such as a powerful magnetic speaker, effective negotiator, loving partner etc. Concentrate this mantra on anything you desire to acquire or develop. You can now read the poem below at your own speed.

"I AM going to become a "*top earning account executive*" because this will enable me to render the world useful service that is needed – and because it will yield me a financial return that will provide me with the necessary material things in life.

I will concentrate upon this desire for ten (10) minutes daily, just before retiring at night and just after rising in the morning, for the purpose of determining how I shall proceed to transform it into reality.

> **I know that I can become a "top earning account executive", therefore I will permit nothing to interfere with my doing so".**
>
> **Signed: by YOU**

**

Bonus tip: Repeat the above statement aloud twice a day for at least 28 days in a row, so that you anchor this new habit. As you may have observed, this easy-to-remember manifestation mantra ties together many ideas that we have already discussed and that are all essential components of your spiritual-preneurship toolkit. Some of these include:

> *constructive habit building*trusting and leveraging your inner power*expressing your unique talents to render useful service*focusing on your passion and definite chief aim*clearly defining what you want to achieve* managing your thoughts etc.*

Our next topic: the SECRET to. . .

***

Unlocking the Law of Attraction

There is one misconception floating out there that the movie *the Secret* may have wrongly introduced, and which needs to be corrected. Some may erroneously believe that whatever you desire in life can be simply attracted. On the contrary: the key to living the life of your dreams is to consciously create it. You do not attract the life of your dreams; you create it! In other words, it is up to you to take full responsibility in designing the destiny that you seek. And you do so by first becoming aware of your limitless inner power. As Deepak Chopra remarks on this topic, "self-power is true power. Self-power is permanent because it is based on the knowledge of the Self". And it is this self-power that is another key to leveraging the natural *Law of Attraction*. As Deepak further explains, one of the key characteristics of your self-power is that, if properly focused, it can draw and magnetize to you "people, situations, and circumstances to support your desires. This is also called support from the laws of nature". All you are required to do is act. The universe does want your active participation in building the life of your dreams, and so does your higher Self. Take this message to heart and remember that we are all on this planet to become the conscious co-creators of our lives!

Interestingly, it is your active participation in the form of massive inspired action that kicks the *Law of Attraction* into even a higher gear! Do you recall?

Success, happiness, health or anything else that you have set out to get is only a decision away! Trust that once you make that decision and take appropriate action, the universe will respond in kind and assist you by orchestrating the right set of circumstance. And the most ironic thing: you have been a part of this natural and automatic process of co-creation all this time, but you were most likely not aware. Now that you have awaken to a few important truths, imagine the power that is now at your creative disposal.

For those only vaguely familiar with this universal principle, "the *Law of Attraction* is a law of nature that is as impartial as the *Law of Gravity*" (Byrne). And from a spiritual standpoint, 'law' can be defined as a process by which the un-manifest becomes the manifest. Based on this law, we attract what we focus on and what matches our vibrational frequency. It is the 'like attracts like' principle. How does this work in real life? As noted in our earlier discussion, if you are angry, you will attract more situations that match the frequency of your anger. If you are happy and feeling wealthy and abundant, you will attract more of what will give you the same feeling. This is a sister-idea to the *Strangest Secret* that "you become what you think about" the most! The closer the vibrational match, the stronger the magnetic pull. Go test out this concept!

Unfortunately, most of us work the *Law of Attraction* unconsciously to our disadvantage. What I mean is that we work it in the negative. Let me demonstrate through a real-life example. A friend of mine was getting into an industry that was filled with fraud and non-performers. In his initial year, his team was so focused on doing everything not to encounter a fraudulent situation that they ended up running into a few shady scenarios! Fortunately, they did not turn out too costly, but one has to wonder if they partly co-created them by focusing on the negative and subconsciously emanating the energy of worry and fear.

***

Working the Law in the Positive

Consider the *Law of Attraction* as another manifestation tool in your spiritual toolkit. Here are some additional success-accelerator tips that allow you to work this natural principle and its creative power to your advantage. Just set your mind high on a worthy goal!

Develop a positive mental attitude and focus on thinking positive thoughts, activities, events and people. Your daily gestures of gratitude, love and faith will elevate your vibration. If you are creating a product or working on a project and feel happy doing it, stick with it. Feeling good signals that you are thinking positive thoughts. If, on the other hand, you resent what you are currently doing, yet are afraid to make a change, you risk getting pulled into a negative vibrational cycle that will sabotage your results.

Feeling good, happy and abundant is another unlocking mechanism that allows you to work the *Law of Attraction* in the positive. If you seek to manifest abundance, feel abundant first and start acting as wealthy and abundant people do. If you seek happiness, get into the happiness feeling every morning, even if you have to manufacture it a bit at first. Before you know it, genuine happiness will have become your new success habit. This idea is so brilliantly captured in the following quote by William James.

"We don't sing because we are happy, we are happy because we sing".

**

Do not make the mistake of getting this causal relationship in reverse! Act fearless to become fearless! Act confident to become confident! Act with belief to develop belief! In other words, act 'as if' to become 'it'. This is another trick of the co-creation trade!

Last but not least, making an explicit ask related to your desires also unlocks the powers behind the *Law of Attraction*. Are you familiar with the expression "don't ask, don't get" or "ask and it is given"? The ask happens by you formulating and stating your goals and hypnotic intentions. To intensify their creative power, state your desires daily out-loud, but also write them down in your journal, ideally with a blue pen. Let me now explain the color choice. It has been observed, tested and proven that the impressions on your subconscious mind are more powerful and carry greater suggestive power when written down with a blue pen. Your mind is simply more receptive to any messages written in blue, so give it what it needs.

To carry on, Esther and Jerry Hicks discuss this principal idea of making an explicit ask to the universe in their popular book titled *Ask and It is Given: Learning to Manifest Your Desires*. They suggest that even if it is just a question that you have, get into the habit of assigning it to your subconscious mind. Then quiet your conscious mind through meditation or another suitable means and listen for the intuitive mind to provide guidance or whisper you the answer. It may take some practice to get to this point, but it is absolutely worth it! As you will see later, spiritual-preneurs regularly cultivate an effective communication with their inner Self.

Here is a quick and easy tip to get you started. Assign the following conscious task to your subconscious: before going to bed at night, ask your subconscious mind to wake up at a specific time in the morning. Do not set the alarm that day and let your subconscious mind to serve as one. As you are assigning the task, focus your mind on that specific wake-up time for at least 30 seconds; 68 seconds is even more ideal. By the way, my subconscious has never failed to wake me up.

***

The Proof is in the Pudding

Despite of it all, I have to confess that I was initially a bit skeptical about some of this material. At some level, it ran against the way that I was trained and brought up. My dad was a Lieutenant Colonel in Slovak Army and my mom was a biology teacher. I grew up in a very pragmatic and fact-based environment, which served me well up to that point. But then my inner voice told me to keep an open mind and experiment some more! The more I "worked" these principles, the more empowering results I'd witness. My initial doubts faded away, my belief went up and my life started to unfold with more ease and contentment. Here is one more personal anecdote on how we leveraged the *Law of Attraction* and along with other natural principles to our benefit.

Several years back, my partner and I were looking for some seed capital to invest in a joint venture project in South America. We had about 2 months to secure the sum of $80,000 or the "80K" needed by May. Getting inspired by an incredibly beautiful sunset on a cruise in the Caribbean, I started humming to myself the following: "80K in May". This catchy phrase must have lodged itself deep within my subconscious and sent out a powerful vibration to the universe. I kept repeating this phrase, focused on the project and visualized a successful resolution in my mind. I also internally aligned myself with the feeling of being already in possession of the $80,000 needed.

Here comes the magic! About seven weeks later, I received a letter from a financial institution about a miscalculation I made on a principal investment made several years ago. My interest payout came to about $80,000. Please note that this money did not just magically appear in my account. It was a result of the habit of saving, some action taken (investing the money) and some universal magic!

While experimenting with the various success principles discussed herein, I manifested an incredible life partner, a fulfilling and lucrative entrepreneurial career, and many other goals and intentions that I have set for myself over the years. By persistently leveraging the information that I am sharing with you, our team managed to penetrate an industry that seemed almost impenetrable to new entrants at first. But that is a story for another book. Taking appropriate action on my end, I also attracted opportunities to live in exotic places and travel the world. I lived in several countries including Panama and have visited over 200 cities in the last 5 years, with most recent trips focused on Asia. I do work seven days a week, but I do it because my work fulfills me. The truth is, I have never felt better about my life, where I currently stand and all the difference and impact that I know I have the power to make. It is my wish that my humble story inspires you to do something personally meaningful and greatly impactful.

I now leave you with another phrase that I happen to use frequently, as it somehow relieves any pressure around your achievements or whatever you are trying to do. It may sound counter-intuitive at first, but it is indeed quite powerful! In fact, it is another manifestation 'acceleration' lever, as it carries with it the idea of staying detached from the final outcome. I picked it up at a leadership event in San Diego and it always seems to conveniently pop up in my mind before an important meeting or an event. What's the magic sentence?

"Care, but not that much!"

One more word of advice before we move on: remain optimistic in all your endeavors, but also plan for challenges and setbacks. As you know from your own experience, no one's journey is void of roadblocks. We all have specific "growth" lessons to go through, as we climb our own mountain of success. More importantly, mastering these challenges is what will set you apart from the rest! As a close friend and a spiritual-preneur remarked:

"Accomplished are not those who were spared, but those who overcame their own challenges on their own path to success".

***

Your Spiritual-MBA Toolkit: Breaking Your Personal Ceiling

The spiritual-MBA toolkit gives you the power-tools that you need to master some of the challenges that you may face. If you apply these tools consistently, they have the potential to break your personal ceiling and lead you to a lifetime of happiness and achievements.

The spiritual MBA toolkit contains various success-building habits, self-leadership and management tactics, as well as other powerful tools that will help you overcome any internal resistance that you may encounter on your way to the top. This toolkit translates into a specific code of conduct that spiritual-preneurs embody and exemplify on a daily basis. This code of conduct is summarized in the *Spiritual-Preneurship Manifesto* below.

SPIRITUAL-PRENEURSHIP MANIFESTO

Bountiful **Giving**. Give freely, frequently and in abundance to put yourself in the flow.

Limitless **Gratitude**. Be grateful for what you have and eager for more.

Unwavering **Faith**. Have faith in the universe, yourself and the unquestionable exactitude with which the universal principles work.

Clarity of Mind. Know what you want and clear your mind of negative thoughts, beliefs and other energetic clutter.

Total **Detachment**. Care, but not that much. Stay detached from the final outcome and flexible about the channel through which your desires come about.

Positive **Mindset**. Feel good and send out positive high-vibrating thoughts and emotions such as love, joy and happiness. A favorite personal affirmation of mine:

I am Love! I am Abundance! I am Joy!

Affirmative Mindset. See yourself already having that which you are after or "assume the feeling of a wish fulfilled" (Neville Goddard).

Be **comfortable** with financial **wealth**. Develop a solid relationship with money or the 'dollars-want-me' mentality. Money comes to people that appreciate it, are comfortable with it and know how to make it work for them and others. They use wealth to create even more wealth.

Know your **Wealth** Creation **Profile**. Cultivate your unique talents and know your wealth creation profile. This is your specific money-making pattern that aligns best with what you are inherently good at, your built-in patterns and natural dispositions.

Spiritually-inspired **habits**. Build constructive success habits that allow you to nurture a deep connection and communication with your higher Self. This includes habits such as mindful meditation, hypnosis, visualization, moments of complete silence etc.

Awareness of **your life path**. Know your life path number and increase your awareness of your specific set of challenges and opportunities related to your life path that you need to overcome and leverage as you climb your own summit of success.

Focus on **being** rather than constantly DOING.

The above list can be easily expanded upon. For the purpose of our discussion, I chose to focus on those areas that made the greatest impact to me personally. Let's now take a closer look at these spiritually-inspired tools, behaviors and mindsets.

***

Karmic Giving & Gratitude

Did you ever observe this very simple fact that you never run out of that which you give freely? Be it books, food, clothes, money, love, compassion etc. It is because when you give, you are riding the wave of another universal principle and that is the *Law of Giving and Receiving*. Dr. Joe Vitale, the author of the international #1 best-seller titled *Spiritual Marketing*, recommends that we all "give daily, give freely, happily and without expectation"! Deepak Chopra adds to this point:

"The universe operates through a dynamic exchange . . . giving and receiving are different aspects of the flow of energy in the universe.

And in our willingness to give that which we seek, we keep the abundance of the universe circulating in our lives".

**

The *Law of Giving and Receiving* is another natural law we need to live by in order to manifest the abundance we seek. According to Deepak Chopra, "the best way to put this law into operation is to make a decision that any time you come into contact with someone, you give them something". This is because abundance is a universal circuit and your giving puts you in a state of continuous flow of abundance. Did you know that the word 'affluence' is derived from the word 'affluere', which means 'to flow in abundance'? On a similar note, the word 'currency' comes from a Latin word 'currere', which means 'to run' or 'to flow'. Think of money and financial wealth as a renewable resource that comes to you freely and in abundance.

An important point to remember is that your karmic giving does not have to be material. A simple smile, compliment, prayer, a good deed or anything else that you have the ability to give will do the trick! Give anything that you are able to, so that you start the engine of the universal process of circulation. Besides giving financially, my daily karmic giving routine entails making someone smile, giving at least one compliment, and performing at least one good deed unexpectedly.

On the subject of giving, I recently saw a movie that depicted a fascinating story of an America tobacco heiress Doris Duke. Born in 1912, she became the richest girl in America when her father passed down a family fortune of over $100 million dollars, and that was over a hundred years ago! A few months after watching the *Bernard and Doris* movie starring Susan Sarandon, my partner and I made an erroneous turn on our last trip to Newport Rhode Island that serendipitously brought us right in front of Doris's family summer estate. We found out while taking a tour that the entire family fortune, including the Newport mansion, was given away to the *Preservation Society of the Newport County* and the *Doris Duke Foundation*. A few million dollars also went to her personal butler Bernard.

Here is the take-away: Give that which you want to acquire! If you put giving first, you will end up with opportunities that make your giving and even more giving possible! I urge you to get into the habit of karmic giving or what Dr. Joe Vitale (Mr. Fire) refers to as "spiritual marketing" and what Phineas Taylor (P.T.) Barnum called "profitable philanthropy. In case you are not familiar, P.T. Barnum was an American showman, politician, businessman and a marketing and publicity genius. His life was recently portrayed in a Hugh Jackman stellar musical *The Greatest Showman*. In closing, spiritual-preneurs give frequently and in abundance and the universe returns their prosperity and generosity mindsets multiplied!

GRATITUDE

Gratitude is an attitude and another essential tool of your spiritual toolkit. It is your appreciative attitude that attracts more things, developments, situations, and people to be grateful for. The attitude to adopt is to be thankful for what you have, yet eager for more. Going back to our gardening analogy, if you attend to your garden gratefully, you will be satisfied with and grateful for the outcomes of your gardening efforts. Why is gratitude so important? The feeling of appreciation increases your vibrational frequency, which magnifies your creative power. Have you ever bought a gratitude rock and every time you looked at it, you thought of something to be grateful for? To put yourself in the universal flow of abundance, cultivate the habit of feeling gratitude and optimistic anticipation daily. This will also help you build a steady positive response to life or a PRL. PRL is an attitude and a mindset! It is looking at the glass half-full, not half-empty. It is about appreciating the lemons that you were given and acting with a relaxed anticipation, commitment and detachment while you make, market and sell your lemonade!

A highly recommended rewarding morning routine is to name three things that you are grateful for at that point in time. Do this for an entire month daily to turn this morning ritual into an automatic success habit. Another fun and easy gratitude habit is to say or write 'thank you' as many times in the day as you possibly can. Did you know that every time you do so, you are again raising your energetic vibration? So, say 'thanks' plenty and reap your energetic rewards daily!

***

The Magic of Believing: Unparalleled Faith

In order to see your efforts materialized, all of your beliefs have to be aligned. Only then will you be able to catch a glimpse of the 'miraculous' unfold in your own life. This includes your beliefs about Self and your abilities, about the nature of the universe, and your degree of deservingness when it comes to the life that you envision for yourself. Stated plainly, you have to have the outmost faith that you can achieve your goals, that you deserve to live the life of your dreams and that the inherently abundant universe is there to assist you every step of the way. Even if your current circumstance may not make any sense! Your belief or lack thereof will either make you or break you, the choice is once again yours. As Zig Ziglar cleverly reminds you:

"If you don't live the life that you believe, you will believe the life that you live"!

**

What I came to realize over the course of my journey and where I went partly wrong, is that to manifest and live abundance, you do have to believe in the plentiful nature of the universe. Would you give abundantly to someone who constantly complains and whines? Would you keep rewarding someone who constantly doubts whether there is enough to go around? If you believe in shortage and undersupply, if you doubt that there is enough, why would the universe try to convince you of the opposite? It will mirror your beliefs and send you exactly those circumstances that match your limited perceptions. You may be reading these pages to awaken to the abundant nature of the universe and the limitless power that rests within you. Have faith in yourself and your abilities to bring any level of abundance into your daily reality! One of the success-keys, as we have seen, is to live in tandem with the natural laws of the universe, such as the *Law of Gravity* or the *Law of Karma*.

Clearly, the process of wealth creation, or any creative process for that matter, starts with your thinking that is in turn shaped by your beliefs. For a girl who grew up in a socialist and practical context, feeling inherently abundant took some time to develop. After all, living a life of comfort, convenience and luxury was often viewed as a waste of resources, evoking feelings of guilt. I have included this personal example for one simple reason: to show you that my current set of beliefs and mindsets is very different from the beliefs I inherited as a result of my social and cultural conditioning. My wealth consciousness is just one example of a purposefully cultivated mindset. You too can overcome whatever mental limitations you may be facing at the moment. You have to be honest with yourself first and admit to yourself that your current mindsets may not be serving your goals. You then have to be willing to gradually change the way you think and anchor your newly-formed mindset so that it becomes permanent. The key take-away from this discussion is that you are inherently affluent so start viewing yourself as such and your external world will re-arrange to match this perspective! As Deepak Chopra further remarks:

"Our true nature is one of affluence and abundance. We are naturally affluent because nature supports every need and desire. We lack nothing, because our essential nature is of pure potentiality and infinite possibilities! Therefore, you must know that you are inherently affluent".

**

Spiritual-preneurs cultivate this expanded Higher view that is rooted in their prosperity and abundance mindset. In fact, one of the built-in features of this pocket book is that it exposes your mind to repetitive suggestions around success and achievement. If you keep reading this book over the course of a month, several pages a day, your mind will start to internalize these messages and act upon this new success programming that you are feeding it via this resource.

Have faith in yourself and your unique talents and learn how to create value (for self and others) with the gifts that you were given. We all have a niche; that something that we are better at than anyone else. If you have not found it yet, keep searching because you too were endowed with a unique gift. Furthermore, your belief in what you can do has to be so strong and grounded, that you get out there and act fearless despite any obstacles and challenges that you may encounter. As a mentor of mine once said to me: "one way to achieve is to believe that you know enough to get started." Do not wait for the perfect plan; take the first step and the next one will reveal itself after you have made the initial move. Take appropriate action and faithfully leave the rest to the universe and the universal intelligence. And if you fall along the way, you will soon realize that nothing tragic happens and your temporary setbacks or perceived failures become just another learning lesson on your journey. What do you do if you encounter a major setback? You get up, integrate new learning, and take a more informed step forward.

Detachment: If you Love it, Set it Free

Are you familiar with this saying: "If you love, set it free"? This expression captures the concept of detachment, which is another effective tool in your spiritual-MBA toolkit. It is also another universal principle (law) that runs through the fabric of the universe. The *Law of Detachment* dictates that in order to acquire anything in the physical world, you have to relinquish your attachment to it (Chopra). This doesn't mean giving up your intention to create your desire. What it does mean is releasing any specific expectations around the final outcome. Detaching also ensures that you are not sending out any underlying messages of need, want, or a lack that will ruin your active efforts.

The key is to feel that you can live without whatever it is that you wish to have. In other words, "if it happens, it happens" is the right attitude to have. This stance signals that you trust and envision a satisfying resolution (outcome). At the same time, if your specific desire does not materialize, you know that something even better is on its way to you. I must admit, embracing and living the concept of detachment is not as easy as it is to write about it. I too had my moments with this principle at first. But after a few instances of successful detachment, what followed were rather pleasantly surprising yet unforeseen results (resolutions). Given the multitude of possible combinations of plausible outcomes that your conscious mind could not possibly conceive of, why limit yourself by attaching to one particular outcome? Create some room around your expectations and allow the universe to surprise you a little.

As a side note, the concept of detachment, which means "being at ease with not getting", translates in the world of yoga to 'raga'. Mastering 'raga' takes time, commitment and practice, but it is a powerful way to expedite the manifestation of your dreams and goals and is yet another essential tool of the spiritual-MBA toolkit.

> **"The minute you relinquish your attachment to the result, combining one-pointed intention with detachment, you will have that which you desire".**
>
> ~Deepak Chopra~

**

How are you doing when it comes to this concept? Do you get attached to one specific outcome and struggle with opening up to alternative solutions? I am sure we all can think of at least one example where detaching was almost impossible, and our energetic bodies were signaling want (lack) or even despair. This is never a healthy way to go! If you want something, set the intention and then release, let go!

Let me give you a more specific example. Let's suppose you are looking for the perfect dress for a destination beach wedding, but nothing catches your eye. You have a crystal-clear mental picture of the dress you want, but have no luck finding it. You leave in two days. You let the idea go of a new dress go and detach. You pack your back-up dress and drive to the airport. As you arrive to the resort, the hotel boutique has on display the exact the dress that you had envisioned from the beginning. It is hanging on the window mannequin and has your name written all over it! Remember this story next time you need to find an item urgently. Staying detached is fundamental to your ability to make your intentions manifest faster. As Deepak concludes:

"Anything you want can be acquired through detachment, because detachment is based on the unquestionable belief in the power of your true Self"!

***

Dollars-Want-Me Mentality

Our earlier discussion introduced the idea that spiritual-preneurs have developed the habit of internally aligning with the feeling of 'having already achieved'. In the words of Neville Goddard, they "assume the feeling of a wish fulfilled". I call this 'affirmative mindset', because you are confirming and signaling through your feelings and general disposition that the universe has already granted you your wishes. This stance is especially effective when creating financial wealth. As Emerson observed, "the man is poor who thinks himself poor". So, join other spiritual-preneurs and cultivate the 'dollars-want-me' mentality. A catchy phrase, would you agree? It comes from a brief article published in 1903 by Henry Harrison Brown. This essay holds a special significance, as it was the first utterance of the following thought:

"Each individual has the ability to so radiate his mental forces that causes the dollar to feel him, love him, seek him and thus draw, at will, all things needed for his unfoldment from the Universal Supply".

**

As you may recall from our earlier conversation, money follows your intangible wealth and that is what you need to build first. Part of this foundational work entails developing and nurturing your personal relationship with money. That is right! You heard me correctly! The same way as people do, money wants to have a personal relationship with you! Although this may sound strange at first, money is just another form of energy that wants to feel welcomed, respected, admired, appreciated and put to use.

On a practical level, an easy way to start cultivating a new and healthier relationship with money is to say 'thank you' every time you buy something, pay a bill or donate. As you spend your dollars, feel grateful for whatever service, asset or experience this money is providing for you (i.e. internet, phone, clothes or travel). And appreciate every dollar that went into securing this item or experience for you. In the words of Arnold M. Patent, the author of *You Can Have It All. A Simple Guide to a Joyful and Abundant Life*, "the sole purpose of money is to express appreciation". It certainly does not hurry to those who perceive it negatively and think that money is bad. If financial wealth has been rather elusive on your end, your solution may rest in expanding your wealth consciousness and cultivating a healthier relationship with money.

***

Know Your Wealth Creation Profile

Have you ever done any personality or behavioral assessments like the Myers-Briggs Type Indicator (MBTI)? These tests are often a required component of many MBA and executive leadership development programs. The MBTI for instance is based on Carl Jung's theory of psychological types and indicates your personality preferences along four (4) dimensions.

Where you focus your attention: Extraversion vs. Introversion (E/I)

The way you take in information: Sensing vs. Intuition (S/T)

How you make decisions: Thinking or Feeling (T/F)

How you deal with the world: Judging or Perceiving (J/P)

Your MBTI personality type is a four-letter combination, such as ESTJ. The MBTI assessment is believed to be a fairly accurate predictor of how we interact with others and the world. It also provides an insight into our preferred leadership style, hence its place in many leadership development programs.

Luckily, you do not have to enroll in an MBA to take these tests, as most of them are available independently online. They can be useful in raising your level of self-awareness, which is another critical component of the spiritual-MBA toolkit.

Spiritual-preneurs push their level of self-awareness one step further. In addition to knowing their personality types, they are also aware of their wealth creation profiles. One could argue that wealth creation is an art. The authors and entrepreneurs Roger James Hamilton and Bruce Muzik support this view and claim that we each create value (wealth) differently, along the lines of our individual 'Wealth Dynamics Profiles'. These money-making patterns mirror our unique talents, dispositions and personal preferences. Hamilton and Muzik further argue that if we step outside our natural wealth dynamics profile, our ability to create financial wealth will be hindered until we re-align.

Here are the 8 wealth creation profiles in broad strokes as proposed by Roger J. Hamilton.

1. **CREATOR**: creates PRODUCTS & services
2. **STAR**: builds BRANDS
3. **SUPPORTER**: builds TEAMS
4. **DEAL-MAKER**: a great sense of TIMING

5. **TRADER**: a great sense of upcoming market SHIFTS

6. **ACCUMLATOR**: collects appreciating ASSETS

7. **LORD**: manages multiple CASHFLOWS

8. **MECHANIC**: SYSTEMS thinker

To learn more, get a copy of Roger's book or take the test online (see Appendix A for a complete reference).

The bottom line is that we each have a natural wealth creation pattern that is aligned with our natural tendencies. If we stay within this profile, we create wealth easily. If we step outside of this profile, our path to financial freedom may present more challenges.

***

What Spiritual-Preneurs Really Do

"Give me a long enough lever, and I can move the Earth".

~Archimedes~

The various tools found in the spiritual-MBA toolkit are your success levers. It is up to you to reach for them and put them to use. This is what successful leaders and entrepreneurs, including spiritual-preneurs, do! In 1999, the *Harvard Business School Press* published a leadership article written by John Kotter titled *What Leaders Really Do*! I remember this article very clearly from my days in executive education, as it was one of the first written discussions on the subject of leadership that made a distinction between two very distinct functions that leaders are asked to perform: the act of managing, and the act of leading. My goal here is not to provide the article summary, but to use it to broaden the scope of our conversation.

In addition to the traits and behaviors already discussed, what else do successful spiritual-MBA-preneurs do differently that puts them in the universal flow abundance and the so-called success continuum?

And more importantly, what can YOU do differently to put yourself in this continuous prosperity and happiness cycle? As an accomplished spiritual-preneur-friend once kindly suggested:

"Do what I do, and you will have what I have"!

***

Spiritual Self-Leadership

Besides knowing how to harness the power of your mind and work in tandem with the spiritual laws of the universe, your ability to lead yourself is your next critical success factor. Self-leadership is about drawing out your inner powers and gifts systematically and deploying your unique set of talents to render useful service and make an impact. Strong self-leadership is a critical success lever, because the most important person that you will ever have to lead in life is yourself. In fact, how can you be entrusted to lead others effectively or anything else for that matter, if you are a poor leader of yourself? It requires self-leadership to craft a new vision, implement an action plan, bring about any kind of change, re-program your mind for success and happiness. This is what Napoleon Hill has to say on the topic of initiative and personal leadership, both required to turn dreams to goals and goals into reality.

"Having chosen a definite chief aim as my life-work, I now understand it to be my duty to transform this purpose into reality. Therefore, I will form the habit of taking some definite action each day that will carry me one step nearer the attainment of my definite chief aim. I know that procrastination is a deadly enemy for all who could become leaders in any undertaking".

Grab Good Habits, Kick the Bad Ones

> "For things in your life to change, you have to change things in your life".

Sounds pretty simple, doesn't it? The truth is, change is easier to talk about than to implement because we are all creatures of habit. It is easy to see how habits can either make you or break you, depending on which ones you choose to add to your self-leadership toolkit. As Zig Ziglar points out:

> **"Good habits are hard to acquire, but easy to live with. Bad habits are easy to acquire, but hard to live with. Nevertheless, we build character from the bricks of habit that we pile up day by day".**

The most insidious thing about destructive habits is that they can creep up on us fast and we often become aware only when we are already enslaved. Some of us literally throw our life away by acquiring and feeding the wrong habits for the most part of our lives. To this point, a Canadian book illustrator John Howe observes:

> **"What a folly to dread the thought of throwing away life at once, and yet have no regard of throwing it away by parcels and piecemeal".**

We do not realize that who we are today is a result of the habits and thoughts that we chose to entertain yesterday. Or as Zig Ziglar puts it:

"After we make the habits, our habits make us"!

Now here is a useful tip. Since bad habits cannot be fully eliminated, you have to replace them with new desired behaviors. Let me give you a scientific piece of evidence for the sake of reference. Brain research has shown that that it takes somewhere between 28 to 31 days of daily repetitive action for new neuropathways to form in your brain. Once these new pathways are created, your new behavior (new habit) has a certain degree of 'stickiness' to it. Do you now see why I suggested that you read this book over a period of 28 days? But, for your new behavior to become fully anchored in your subconscious and become automatic, you need to stick with it for about 2 months, or 66 days to be exact (James Clear, Appendix A).

Now let's suppose you decide to cut your mindless TV watching time or another unproductive habit and replace it with a regular reading routine. You decide to read an hour each evening after dinner. To build and sustain this habit successfully, hold yourself accountable to your new reading schedule for a month and preferably two, as per the above scientifically-grounded suggestion.

Your take-away: Choose your habits wisely. Define your new vision for self and then align your habits accordingly. Make sure that your habits are bringing you closer to, and not further away from, your dreams and goals. Luckily, you are already ahead of the game by the virtue of buying this book! I am about to give you an overview of key success habits that spiritual-preneurs consciously cultivate and that you too can add to your self-leadership toolkit. Habits work the same way as your gardening: you have to periodically weed out the 'unwanted' and plant a new and more valuable seed, which in this case is a new constructive habit.

At your own leisure, I encourage you to conduct an honest inventory of your current habits. If you are not where you want to be in life, maybe your current habits are not supporting the achievement of your goals. We all need to self-correct at times, as no one is perfect. I have to confess, I had to overcome the habit of breaking agreements that I would make to myself. Little did I know that this bad habit was eating away at my positive self-image. Ask yourself! How can you view yourself as an effective leader, if you don't always follow up on your promises made to self or others? As with all success-compromising habits, the first step toward transformation is becoming aware. The second step consists in taking responsibility and corrective action. To this point, the spiritual-MBA toolkit is your roadmap to building empowering and success-driving habits.

***

Leverage the Now

> "**Yesterday is history, tomorrow is a mystery, today is a gift, which is why we call it the present**".
>
> *~Bill Keane~*

Spiritual-preneurs have developed a heightened level of awareness of the creative power of the present moment. They also practice the habit of being present and staying focused on the right-here and right-now. They realize the value of the present moment and do not waste it by overanalyzing events of the past or overthinking what will be. As the famous song by Doris Day goes: "Que sera, sera, whatever will be, will be"! The only thing that is certain and can be leveraged is the present moment. More importantly, it is in the 'now' that you can fully access your inner power, so why choose to be anywhere else?

Some of you may be familiar with this concept through Eckhart Tolle's book titled *The Power of Now: A Guide to Spiritual Enlightenment*. Eckhart is a German spiritual teacher, philosopher and a writer. Before writing his best-sellers and realizing his broader calling, Eckhart spent about two years on a park bench in a severely depressed state, pondering the meaning of existence. According to Eckhart Tolle, the present moment or the 'now' is so powerful for one simple reason. If we fully and whole-heartedly focus on what's in front of us now, we do not have the time or the energy to be consumed by regrets of the past or worries and fears of the future. Our intense focus on what is makes the 'now' void of all problems. Think about it. Or even better, think of something that you love to do, one of your hobbies for instance. Imagine yourself performing this leisure activity right now, fully present and immersed, doing under the perfect set of circumstances and in total joy. You know that you are fully present when you lose track of time as a result of your intense presence and focus. Michael Csikszentmihalyi, the author of *Flow: The Psychology of Optimal Experience*, believes that it is your passionate focused effort in the present moment that puts you in the state of flow. When this happens, you experience pure joy, happiness and creative fulfillment.

There is one more benefit to staying focused on the present moment. When you are present and in a state of flow, you tend to suspend your incessant thinking generated by your conscious mind. You thus free up energy for more creative endeavors. Being fully immersed and in the 'now' allows you to free your mind from the constant noise and useless chatter that goes on internally and that hijacks and compromises your mental creative power. To this point, Eckhart Tolle believes that humanity as a collective suffers from a disease that he diagnoses as constant overthinking, overuse and over-reliance on our analytical, rational, logical mind that should be used only at certain times, as and when needed. Eckhart Tolle further argues that in most instances, it is to your benefit to turn your left-brain rational thinking off and simply be in the now.

When you allow yourself to fully focus on what is, you literally send yourself a gift. In the now, you can tap into your creative energy and thus allow yourself to be the creator that you are meant to be! You free yourself to create because your logical mind is not fixated on solving any problems or projecting negative future scenarios. To be frank, Eckhart's book made me realize what a slave I was to my rational mind. My awareness was followed by a conscious decision to make a change. A decision to live fully in the present creative moment as much as possible, while leveraging my logical, analytical and rational mind as needed. This is about 25% of the time and includes activities such as creating and analyzing plans and strategies for the future, comparing courses of action and any other analytical work.

Your take-away: stay in the 'now' as much as possible, as it is the only powerful creative moment. While this may take conscious effort and practice, it is a rewarding habit to build. Get into the habit of being present and focused on the task at hand and nothing else. Here is my final argument that underscores the importance and the power of the present moment.

"Nothing is there to come, and nothing past. But an eternal NOW does always last".

~Abraham Cowley~

What's my point? Many spiritual gurus and meta-physicists agree that time as we know it is an illusion and the only moment that counts is now. Since I am not a philosopher or an expert in metaphysics, I will defer to a more credible source to expand your view on this topic. For instance, Einstein's math teacher Hermann Minkowski proved the following through mathematical equations:

"All the past and future of an individual person all meet at a single point. All events in the universe are all occurring simultaneously in this eternal moment of now"!

**

Knowing how powerful the present moment is, do not waste it! Figure out what you want, create a plan and do at least one thing each day that will bring you closer toward its achievement. Most importantly, be sure to act the moment you feel inspired. Moments of inspiration are whispers sent to you by a higher power and should not be ignored. We will revisit this concept in more detail shortly, as it is another spiritual self-leadership tool and a success habit.

***

Take Massive & Bold Action

The second component to leveraging the power of the present moment is taking immediate massive action. Action means growth and it is rewarded in the world.

Non-action leads to stagnation and runs against the very fabric of the universe. But know this! The rewards that you reap for your life's actions are determined based on the precise workings of the *Law of Compensation*. This is yet another immutable universal law, which dictates that in life, "you get what you deserve or what is commensurate with the effort that you put out" (Napoleon Hill). You may feel at times that you deserve better than what you have acquired, but your compensation is always in a direct proportion to your actions and efforts undertaken. Live each moment fully and successfully, because your life is a collage of countless individual moments occurring in the now.

Let's try something out: Why not start building the habit of taking inspired action right now? Stop reading and if you are free to do so, go do the one thing that you have been meaning to do for a while but that you have been putting off for days, weeks or months. There is always that one first obvious step that will get your own success momentum going, but it is up to you to take that first step. So, think about what that one action step could be and go do it! Perhaps this quote by Vance Havner will help jumpstart your efforts.

> **"It is not enough to stare up the steps, unless you also step up the stairs"!**

***

Ride the Idea-Wave: Inspired Creation

Let me ask you this: can you tell me what is the most spiritual aspect behind the power of now that we just discussed? I'll let you in on another secret shared by many spiritual gurus. Each inspirational idea or a thought that comes to you has its own burst of creative energy attached. What's the practical implication? If you act immediately when the idea comes to you and when you feel inspired, you will get to ride your idea's energetic wave, leveraging this injection of new energy. As a reward and a result of acting on the idea quickly, the universe pushes you forward, and your idea is building rapid forward momentum.

Dr. Joe Vitale, a spiritual guru and best-selling author mentioned earlier, offers a unique spiritual perspective on the subject. He is of the view that in order to ensure that ideas are acted upon, the universe inspires more than one person with the same creative idea simultaneously. This is the universe's insurance policy to guarantee that the idea is acted upon by someone and is physically manifested. To illustrate this point, let's assume that five people were inspired with the same idea to launch an online business. Out the five people involved, two will ignore the idea altogether, one will think about it and do nothing, one will make one attempt and stop there, and the fifth person is the one who will work the idea until he or she succeeds. To no one's surprise, it is usually the person who acts the fastest, the one who acts now and who perseveres. My observations of other successful spiritual-preneurs made me see that they have learned to seize this "first-mover-advantage" and turned it into another success habit. Remember this 'golden nugget' next time you feel inspired to do something. How many times do we come across a new product or a service and we tell ourselves: "I had the same or a similar idea!" Do you see what I mean?

Let's get even more spiritual to drive this point home. Inspired action is a result of an inspiration that comes from a higher power in the form of an intuitive nudge or what Oprah calls a whisper. Inspired action is joyous and happens in this moment. In this moment of inspiration, you are guided by your intuition rather than your rigid analytical mind. This circles back to Eckhart's suggestion above; we need to learn how to turn our rational and logical mind off when we don't need it. However, our ability to hear this whisper is not guaranteed without some initial groundwork. You have to center yourself, calm the chatter of your conscious mind and get clear. Keep on reading to discover what getting clear means, as nothing happens without it!

Without a doubt, spiritual-preneurs have developed the habit of taking immediate action and profit from riding the energy of their inspired ideas. They are well aware of how the process of deliberate creation really works. They know that they do not need a perfect plan to start, nor do they need to know each successive step in advance. They know that what matters most is taking that first immediate step. And what do you next? You go as far as you can see, and when you get there, the next steps will be revealed. Imagine yourself on the road driving to a preselected destination. You may not be able to see your end-point, but you can see each successive turn clearly. The same happens in any undertaking. When you take the step that is in front of you, the next one will reveal itself and you will know where to go and what to do from that point on. Here is my simple belief:

"Imperfect action beats inaction any minute"!

Why are so many of us hung up on having to know each step before we take any action? It is partly due to our formal schooling that conditions us to focus most of our time on perfecting our plans, techniques and strategies or the 'how'. While mastering techniques and crafting well thought-out plans is an important step, I am of the view that our formal training, including our formal education, does not devote sufficient amount of time to the more important questions of 'what' (goals, intentions) and 'why' (reasons) or the crucial questions of 'why we do what we do'! This is a concept called a "training balance scale" that I became familiar through a network of like-minded entrepreneurs. The 'what' part of the scale refers to your thoughts, goals, desires, attitudes, mental processes, vibration, energy, emotions. This is where your training scale most likely needs some rebalancing, as the 'what' and 'why' dimensions is where the majority of your inner work needs to be done. The 'how' becomes for now secondary.

Bottom line: As much as you do need a plan in life to succeed, make sure you do not get too bogged down by its rigidity and remain flexible, adaptable and open-minded. As a personal tip, I find my strategy and planning work leads to more creative and satisfying solutions (and business proposals) when I engage both the analytical and logical left-side as well as the creative, artistic and intuitive right-side of the brain. One quick and easy way of stimulating your creative subconscious mind is by listening to some classical music, such as baroque.

Become Better or Surrender

Are you committed to a process of life-long learning and personal and professional growth? Or are you happy that you are done with school once and for all? I doubt that is your case, since you bought this self-development book and are almost half-way through. It does not take a genius to figure out that to climb the ladder of success and reach the top, you must have the eagerness and curiosity to learn and grow!

I once read in an entertainment magazine of a man who developed a rather unique and creative habit to ensure that he would learn something new on a regular basis. Every year, he made a new friend that had to meet one simple condition: he or she had to be a few years younger than the friend that he had made the previous year. As this man was getting older, his social circle that he was building around him was getting younger. This created a win-win dynamic! The youngsters learned from the wise-old man and he in turn got an injection of some youthful energy and learned about the latest trends from the youth that kept him more relevant. My 92-year old auntie Mary always feels more alive after I visit. And she does learn something new from me ever time; she just quickly forgets she did! May she be blessed!

The point is, making friends with people outside your normal social circle has hidden benefits. I get much joy and satisfaction from spending time with my 10-year old niece Maiya and her little brother Owen. Our time together recalibrates my playfulness scale. The funny thing is, I always get inspired with great ideas after some quality-time with these two munchkins. Bottom line: in order to reach the top of your own summit, you have to keep bettering yourself every day. Or surrender to a mediocre and unrewarding existence. As Robert Collier observes:

"The whole purpose of our existence is growth. Life is dynamic, not static. The one unpardonable sin of nature is to stand still and to stagnate".

**

From this perspective, complacency and procrastination are your enemies. Set your intention to go from good to great. Know that you have the potential and all of the necessary skills to go from an average, monotone existence to a fabulously rewarding, abundant and meaningful one. And if you are already happy and have all you need, then help others achieve the same. Set your goals high and start visualizing your new successes daily. And do as W. Clement Stone - a businessman, philanthropist and New Thought self-help book author - encourages us to do:

"Aim for the moon. If you miss, you may hit a star".

Here is even a better variation of the above quote by Norman Vincent Peale.

"Shoot for the moon. Even if you miss, you'll land among the stars"!

PS. Remember that YOU have the lead-role and are the lead-star in your own *Incredible Life* movie premiere! Make sure that you are writing and performing based on the right screenplay! One that is personally meaningful and corresponds to the life that YOU want live!

It goes without saying that your personal development process entails examining and potentially altering some of your ways, approaches, habits, thoughts, beliefs or behaviors. However, your willingness to grow and accept change is what sets you apart. It also helps to connect to the right social network that will encourage you and support your personal development. Fortunately, there is no shortage of social media groups to tap into. I also recommend the old-fashioned in-person conferences and events. It is always refreshing to get out of your local element and meet new people from all walks of life.

Let Life Happen

In line with the *Law of Flexibility*, spiritual-preneurs practice "pragmatic acceptance" of what is, rather than resisting the present moment and everything that it brings. They accept present circumstances, themselves and others and are ready to fully surrender to what is happening at the moment. Let me be clear. Surrender does not mean giving up on life. Quite the contrary, it is realizing that you do not have complete control over what happens. It is admitting at some level that there is an all-knowing and omnipresent power that orchestrates our various life events from a higher perspective. Once you awaken to this realization and accept it, you will be able to relax into life and 'let life happen' without your constant interference, doubting or complaining.

So where does our discussion leave us? Here is your spiritually-inspired blueprint that you should think about modelling: know what you want and tap into your mind power, pull your weight, go with the flow and be flexible, surrender to the present even if you don't like it, and acknowledge that there is a higher power that is the backbone of the universe, whichever name you choose to give it.

As you may recall from our earlier discussion, 'surrender' is the 3rd stage of the awakening process or your journey toward enlightenment and fulfillment. For this reason, it is an essential facet of the spiritual-preneurship and a critical mindset of the spiritual self-leadership toolkit. We all know people who seem to coast through life effortlessly, always enjoying what's in front of them and always progressing and hitting their milestones. What's their secret? In addition to a strong string of success habits, they embrace the concept of surrender and live it. These accomplished spiritual-preneurs approach every circumstance and/or situation with a relaxed attitude, accepting everything about each moment, while keeping an optimistic vision and expectation of what's coming their way.

One last remark on the subject of surrender, which often requires that we undergo some kind of a change. At a very basic level, our actions, behaviors and mental processes are guided by two primary instincts: the possibility of a gain, which we equate with pleasure. The second instinct that guides us is pain or loss avoidance. In other words, we agree to do those things that promise potential gains and avoid those situations and actions where we risk losing or experiencing some painful outcomes. Our unfounded fear of change stems from one critical point: we equate change with the unknown, which brings us back to pain. Look at the equation below.

CHANGE equals UNKNOWN equals potential PAIN equals change AVOIDANCE equals STAGNATION and you know what comes next!

***

From SMART Goals to Hypnotic Intentions

Spiritual-preneurs are effective leaders of self that have formed the habit of setting SMART goals. Have you ever heard of this concept? Let me clarify. The word SMART is an acronym that everyone interested in succeeding needs to become familiar with. SMART goals are smart because they are set effectively ('smartly'), and this very step increases your likelihood of sticking with them and accomplishing them. The acronym SMART simply means that your goals should to be specific, measurable, attainable, realistic and timely. Here is an example of a 'smart' goal: I will exercise three times a week for 45 minutes, which will be further divided into 20 minutes for cardio, 10 minutes for stretching, and 15 minutes for resistance. I will re-assess this routine in 28 days. A rather ineffective way of setting a similar fitness goal would be to say to yourself that you simply want to exercise more. How can you measure your progress in the absence of any tangible (numerical) benchmark? When setting goals and creating action plans, always remember to build-in some flexibility in case of potential setbacks. As you know, things rarely go as planned. Embrace uncertainty, learn how to navigate the unknown and your overall life journey will be more enjoyable.

Here is one more goal-related insight that has been of value to me personally. The process of setting SMART goals is really a chance for you to set yourself up for success from the get-go. What do I mean? Design the rules of your game based on your knowledge of self, setting them smartly so that you are challenged but also set up to win! Let's say your goal is to develop a regular reading habit. If you know you only have 20 minutes a day available to you, do not set your initial reading goal to two hours a day because you will most likely not stick with it and get discouraged. Why would you set yourself up for failure from the outset? Whatever 'smart' goal you are working towards, set your performance benchmark so that you hit your target, build encouragement and collect small wins along the way! For the sake of our discussion, the concept of SMART goals was coined by a well-known Professor of Organizational Psychology, Professor Gary Latham, some leadership development programs during my career at the Rotman School of Management.

Spiritual-preneurs push the concept of SMART goals (focused attention) one step further and enhance their creative power by upgrading their goals into intentions, while working in tandem with other natural laws. As per the *Law of Intention and Desire*, intention is powerful because it transforms. According to Deepak Chopra, "intention triggers transformation of energy and information and organizes its own fulfillment". Therefore, intention is the real power behind your desires. As Deepak puts it, intention is desire without attachment to the outcome.

The term 'hypnotic' intention was coined by the aforementioned spiritual teacher Dr. Joe Vitale. What gives your intentions their hypnotic power and increases their magnetic pull is the intensity of your focus. You also intensify and magnetize your intentions by your ability to repeatedly visualize your successes and feel and act as if you had already achieved. A sure way to make your intentions more hypnotic is to take your first action step within 24-48s hours after setting that intention. Taking some definite action within this timeframe hypnotizes your intentions, because it anchors their messages within your subconscious. Scientific studies have shown that this so-called anchoring takes place in the form of new neuropathways that are formed in your cerebral cortex (brain). If you act on your intention the recommended timeframe, a new neuropathway associated with that intention will form in your brain and this simple step will put you ahead of the game. This neuro path-away acts like a new cerebral highway that will connect you to your intended goal and lead you to the finish line, if kept us through repetitive action.

Here is a recent personal anecdote on the power of intentions. This past summer, my partner and I attended a stunning white party situated in the historic Niagara-on-the-Lake. A wonderful group of friends and business associates joined us that blissful night. There was only one intention I had set before going to the party; aside from having a good time and trying some new local wine. My simple intention for that evening was to come home with a professionally-looking spontaneous photo that would capture the essence of the evening and serve as a lasting memory. I saw the picture vaguely in my mind as the limo picked us up.

It turned out to be a splendid, elegant and fun evening where new friendships were made. Here comes the magical touch of the universe! Right after the main course, as my partner and I stepped into a narrow cobble-stone alley to make a phone call, a woman appeared out of nowhere. Without initiating any conversation, she approached us and insisted that we let her take a few photos of us with the backdrop of a stunning Victorian home that we were leaning against. Does it surprise you that she happened to be a professional photographer? If you are curious to see the photo that the universe had orchestrated for us that evening, please connect with me via social media.

The Trick of the Trade

As emphasized throughout our discussion, spiritual-preneurs are aware of the various subtleties behind their mind's inner workings. To this point, they know well to avoid stating their goals in the negative. What is the underlying reasoning? Your subconscious mind or the engine of your deliberate creation cannot interpret negatives such as 'not' or 'no'. When you use them in the formulation of your goals, they are simply disregarded when your subconscious interprets and processes your messages. Too often, because of the way we articulate our intentions, our mind absorbs and acts on the very opposite of what we are intending to achieve. Such misinterpretation always results in an unwanted outcome. Let me give you an example.

Let's suppose that you want to be financial independent, but you stated your goal as follows: "I don't want to be financially limited". If this is how you state your goal, you will most likely experience some financial pressures or shortages. Why? Based on how you worded your intention, the message that your mind took away and acted upon, after dropping the negative, was: "I want to be limited financially". This is the new message that your mind will act upon and deliver to you in your physical reality. The correct way to state the same goal is to say:

"I AM financially free! I AM boundlessly abundant! Money comes to me freely and in abundance"!

Your take-away: strip away the negative and state all of your intentions in positive tone and the present tense. This way, you provide your subconscious with the right raw material for its manifestation work. Let me give you one more example to reinforce this point. Fear in its endless forms is the most common enemy for most people. Fear of public speaking, snakes, spiders, heights, airplanes, germs, you name it. What's the best way to word your fear-related intentions?

The INCORRECT way: I do not want to be afraid.

The WINNING way: I AM fearless.

***

Poor Me, Poor Me, Pour Me a Drink!

"It is not your fault, but it is your responsibility to fix whatever is wrong in your life."

~Joe Vitale~

Perhaps this is not what you want to hear and find the above statement a bit harsh, however, it does have an empowering element. It wakes you up to the fact that whatever your life is like at the moment, you have to stop playing the victim and take a 100% responsibility. Furthermore, you have to admit to yourself without feeling angry that you must have contributed to creating your current circumstance. Do you really want to be stuck in stage 1 of the awakening process? Your goal has to be to transcend this stage of victimhood and move toward empowerment and self-realization. Spiritual-preneurs have moved through these stages successfully and act and create from their inner power and the state of empowerment.

So, to sum up our conversation, your first step in moving forward in your life in more noticeable and transformational ways is to acknowledge and accept that you have helped to create everything that you are currently experiencing. You need to assume full responsibility for who you are and where you currently stand. You also have to fully commit to do whatever it takes to get back on track. You can start by implementing these spiritually-inspired self-leadership principles. Moreover, your very decision to take full responsibility gets you energetically unstuck. Success is only a decision away! A word of caution: do not allow any feelings of guilt or remorse creep up as you start reflecting upon your life more deeply. These destructive energies will only intensify your victimhood mentality and keep you stuck in this vicious cycle. Reflect, create a plan and move on! And most importantly...

Follow the Ball Through!

Staying accountable and seeing your actions, projects or initiatives through is another key success habit of spiritual-preneurs and anyone who succeeds. It is worth noting that there is a two-fold accountability at play here: being accountable to yourself and to others or the external world. And both require respecting the agreements you make. Why is this so important? Your word should be your bond, otherwise, you are compromising your integrity and creating unnecessary reputational risk for yourself. On a secondary note, breaking agreement shows very little respect towards yourself and others. Even worse, your failure to follow through takes your power away and sabotages your efforts to reach the top of your personal summit.

Here is one more repercussion of not seeing things through and relapsing on your promises. These two pesky habits have can have a negative impact on your self-image. Just think about it logically. How can you entertain a positive image of yourself, if you never do what you say you are going to do? And how can others take you seriously? Breaking agreement diminishes your personal and professional credibility and generates low vibrating emotions, such as regret and guilt. This puts a spoke in your success wheel, so to speak, and throws you in a 'non-action' pattern and potential paralysis. This is the opposite of the success momentum that spiritual-preneurs find themselves in.

Bottom line: not following through reverses your forward momentum. For those familiar with astrology, compare the consequences of breaking agreements to getting stuck in never-ending phases of planetary retrogrades. If the image scares you a bit, then make sure that when you say you will do something, you actually do it! It is that simple!

As referenced earlier, one crucial strategy that spiritual-preneurs rely on to ensure proper follow-through is having a plan of attack in case of potential setbacks. Having even a vague plan for a potential derailment can mean the differences between persevering or giving up. In other words, always have an alternative plan in mind. It is a matter of being pragmatic and prepared. I look at setbacks as a natural part of any process of growth and development. Setbacks are only temporary and can be leveraged if you have the right mindset. Overcoming potential roadblocks successfully also enhances your self-image and strengthens your confidence in your own abilities. After all, the biggest leaps of growth and some of the most valuable lessons come from skillfully mastering the most difficult of circumstances. Said differently, your character is not defined by ordinary moments, but rather moments of setbacks, disappointment and misfortune. What matters most is how you choose to respond to these situations. The words of Robert Cavett sum up perfectly our current discussion.

"Leaders are those who follow through on a decision long after the excitement and the emotion of the moment have passed"!

**

This commitment mindset is another defining feature of spiritual-preneurship. Embrace these success principles, apply the tactics and adopt the new mindsets to witness your current performance ceiling elevate. To your benefit, you have quite the repertoire of tools available in your spiritual leadership toolbox and we are only part-way through our discussion. In the remaining chapters, each topic is supplemented with practical and implementable take-aways or success primers. If applied consistently, these success tips have to potential to help you narrow the gap between where you currently are in life and where you envision yourself to be. Here is your first success primer.

Subject: BREAKING AGREEMENTS

If you break an agreement with either yourself or others, you need to take an immediate remedial action to negate the effects of this faux-pas. This entails two things: you have to acknowledge that you disrespected your word, and you have to apologize for it. The act of acknowledgement alone will release blocked energy that was created as a result of the agreement violation. You may be surprised to learn that your apology alone will clear your energetic field of any debris or negativity that was created when you broke your promise. Bottom line: your apology is required energetically so that you can move forward. This scenario shows that not everything that is happening is always visible to the naked eye.

If thoughts of promises broken are popping into your head as you read this paragraph, make a list and start with your apologies! It will not only clear your energetic field, but also replenish some of the power that you gave away when you disrespected yourself. On a final note, breaking agreements is simply not taking responsibility and not having the necessary discipline and self-control. All of this can be remedied with one simple step: consistent application of tools, strategies and mindsets found in your spiritual-MBA toolkit!

***

Born to Win Self-Image

Looking at the habit of follow-through from the other end, your likeliness to finish what you started is very much dependent on how you view yourself and how robust and healthy is your self-image. Spiritual-preneurs holds a strong and winning image of themselves and always sees things through. They know that breaking agreements is detrimental to their self-image and can lead to stagnation and potential self-sabotage. Here is another tip: you have two ears and one mouth so use them proportionately. And if you say that you are going to do something, put your money where your mouth is! Plain and simple.

Successful spiritual-preneurs strengthen their already healthy self-image by a strong belief in their abilities to achieve even the boldest goal. They live by Napoleon Hill's credo that "if you believe, you will find a way to achieve". They practice positive self-talk and program for success through empowering affirmations (Appendix C). Here is one such affirmation that definitely ranks high on its stickiness factor.

Every DAY, in every WAY, I AM getting BETTER and BETTER!

***

What Winners Actually Do: Mirror, Mirror!

Do you sometimes feed your mind with negative suggestions? Get in the habit of positive self-talk! Let me show you another useful success building technique that spiritual-preneurs use frequently to reinforce their self-image. I am talking about the mirror technique introduced by Claude Bristol in his entertaining and insightful pocket book the *Magic of Believing*.

Here is the mirror technique with the exact set of instructions. Stand in front of a mirror where you can see yourself at least waist up. Stand straight and take a few deep breaths in and out. Keep breathing until you "feel a sense of power, strength and determination" come over you (Bristol). Next, look yourself deeply in the eyes and tell yourself that you are going to get what you are after, then name it aloud. Speak with force and conviction and declare your total belief in your ability to attain your goal. Use this technique at least once a day and stick with it for at least a month (28 days) before you judge its effectiveness in helping you realize your goals.

You can also apply some creativity and combine the mirror technique with Napoleon Hill's manifestation mantra. The key is to have fun with the process and remain playful, imaginative and intuitive. This technique has a direct application in any field including business and can be an excellent success primer before any important meeting or a sales presentation. After all, if you do not sound convincing to yourself in the mirror, how can you expect to convince anyone else to buy your product or service? The key thing in working with the mirror technique properly is to make sure that all of your statements are articulated out-loud. Are you wondering why? The scientific community has proven that speaking aloud sends more powerful messages to your subconscious than when you whisper in your mind. Quite simply, by looking at yourself in the mirror while speaking, you increase the vibration and the force by which the meaning of your words penetrates to your subconscious mind (Bristol).

***

What Winners Actually Do: The Pose of a Champion

Let's now go back to the animal kingdom and allow me to ask you another question. What do primates like chimpanzees do if they win in a fight with another primate? Animals pound their chests with closed wrists a few times. What about us, humans? Is there a universal pose or a non-verbal gesture associated with winning? What would a marathon runner do, when hitting the finish line and scoring Olympic gold? What would you if you just found out you were hired by your dream company or accepted by the school of your choice? What winning gesture would you most likely perform? My guess, you would most likely raise your arms up in victory into a V-like shape and jump up, especially if you are the enthusiastic type. The interesting thing is that the effectiveness of this 'pose of a champion' has been tested in a controlled behavioral study that was presented a TED Talk Event (Appendix A).

Here is more about the experiment and its findings. Two groups of students were asked to participate in this study. Subjects of both groups were asked to take 90 seconds to prepare for an interview. Behavioral responses of both groups were recorded and then analyzed. The control group was given no special set of instructions and the participants were asked to do what they would normally do in preparation for an interview. The video recordings of the 90-second segment showed most of the participants in this group either hunched over at their desk, with legs crossed, heads down, nervously anticipating the interviewer's questions and silently mulling over potential answers.

On the contrary, participants of the experimental group were given a very specific set of instructions. They were asked to spend this 90-second period with their hands up in a V-like shape, holding a clear visual image of them succeeding at the interview. What did the study reveal? As you may have guessed, the experimental group by far outperformed the control group. This study confirmed that the application of this simple pose of a champion led to a significantly better performance during the interview. Together with the visualization technique, it strengthened participants' self-image and sent a strong message and intention of winning to their subconscious. This set an overall winning tone and victory followed.

***

C+3P Equals Success Momentum

Successes of spiritual-preneurs are partly driven by the following formula.

SUCCESS equals COMMITTMENT plus PERSISTENCE. PERSEVERANCE. PATIENCE.

This success equation has a universal application and it been inspired by our business experiences in Asia. Our successes in this part of the world would not have been possible without our C+3P approach. As a famous Chinese proverb goes:

"Patience is power. And with time and patience, the mulberry leaf will become silk"!

**

Spiritual-preneurs know how to leverage this self-reinforcing abundance & success building cycle. It is really the opposite of the vicious self-sabotaging cycle that bad habits can pull us into. Let's take a closer look at what the 'success momentum' really is and how you can easily 'slide' into one. Here is an everyday example. You look in your work calendar and notice a high-potential sales call scheduled for tomorrow. As always, you prepare. For whatever reason, you prepare more thoroughly than for any other call and impress the client with your creative and colorful chart and an innovative proposal. The conference call goes remarkably well. You get compliments on your work and secure the client. This positive outcome increases your confidence and bumps up your belief in self. You wonder what else are you capable of. Because of this new client, you have earned yourself a nice Christmas bonus and doubled your sales volume. Your overall level of enthusiasm for your work goes up and you take another massive action that pays off even more! The more success you get, the bolder the actions you take. All of a sudden, you feel confident to take on even riskier projects (within limits) with even greater earning potential. Your vision of what is possible expands, your commitment intensifies, and the success momentum goes on like a merry-go-round!

If you persist with your efforts for a month or two, you will witness the magic of this prosperity cycle for yourself. Bottom line: commitment combined with persistent action, patience and perseverance guarantees remarkable results and leads to victory! It is your commitment to cultivating the right success habits that helps you stay in this success momentum. Make a conscious commitment to work the tools of this spiritual toolkit and you will soon find yourself riding your own success momentum. Just do the right things long enough consistently and watch what happens!

***

Mind Expansion and Your Path to Fulfillment

"A mind that is stretched by experience can never go back to its old dimensions"!

~ Oliver Wendell Holmes Jr. ~

Spiritual-preneurs are aware of this simple fact and take actionable steps to expand their mind and knowledge on a regular basis. They know that from a metaphysical standpoint, their expanded consciousness gives them the ability to literally experience more each moment of every day. While a detailed discussion of consciousness evolution is well beyond the scope of this book and my level of knowledge, there is one clear important message to underscore. The more committed you stay to nurturing and expanding this precious resource of yours - your mind - the more fulfilling and rewarding your life experience will be. Conversely, a closed mind and limited thinking often results in a life of drudgery, boredom and stagnation.

An effective tactic that you can implement to this end is to start consciously increasing the number of empowering images that you expose your mind to daily. The underlying principle is this: the more images related to your goals and visions you imprint onto the canvas of your subconscious mind, the more material your mind has to work with as it starts transforming your desires into their physical counterpart.

COMMUNICATING WITH YOUR VISUAL MIND

Before we talk about some specific mind-expanding techniques such as playful visualization, let me give you three more 'mind facts' to round up your knowledge and our previous discussion. In order to harness the power of this precious asset, you need to understand how to communicate with it effectively.

Mind fact 1: Your mind is 50% visual and therefore responds effectively to visual stimuli. In fact, it stores, records and processes every image it was ever exposed to. It responds by translating the strongest and most emotionalized mental images into physical reality. Science has also supported the fact that your subconscious mind gets faster results when the commands given to it are accompanied by corresponding images of the desired goals. As Ziglar further explains, these images that you present to it "may be faint, sketchy, or even unfinished; even if it is only an outline, it will be sufficient for the subconscious to act upon". What's the practical implication here? Feed your mind with images that serve as a constant reminder of your life's goals and that inspire and empower you to move forward. In line with our movie analogy used throughout this book, you are the screenplay writer, the executive producer, the creative director and the star of your own *Incredible Life* movie. Start perfecting your mental movie sets and make them spectacular! Before you know it, you will be living them in real life. Another useful piece of advice: the more color and contrast your images have, the more impactful their impressions on your subconscious and the greater their creative and transformative power.

Mind fact 2: Your mind cannot tell the difference between what is real and what is imagined. It will take the images that you feed it daily and use them as raw materials when co-creating your physical reality. Let me give you an example. Let's suppose you would like to drive (own or lease) a Jaguar F-Type convertible. Get a clear picture of it in your preferred color and hang it somewhere can see it as many times a day as possible (i.e. your smartphone screen, bathroom mirror, above stove). You can even photoshop yourself into the image if you want to be that creative. Look at the image repeatedly with belief, excitement and optimistic anticipation, while taking appropriate action.

This is where your focus and concentration come in handy. It is through repetitive focus that you hold your desired images steady and embed them within your subconscious. If you integrate playful visualization into your daily wealth creation routine and match it with a genuine feeling and belief, I guarantee that you will be sitting in your new car faster than you otherwise would have. Bottom line: exposing your mind to empowering visual representations of your goals expedites their physical manifestation, provided that all the other success ingredients are in place. If you keep looking at a picture of your new beach house but deep down don't believe it will ever be yours, don't expect this dream to materialize in your outer circumstance.

Mind fact 3: The third mind fact is a word of caution indeed. The images that have the strongest magnetic pull and that your mind acts on the fastest are those mental images that evoke some of the most extreme emotions that we have outlined earlier. This principle is well in line with the *Law of Attraction* and can be leveraged to your advantage if the emotions that you feel are positive (i.e. love, hope). Can you imagine the creative energy of a musician whose passion for artistic expression runs through him like a powerful waterfall?

The real culprit when it comes to your manifestation efforts are any negative emotions (i.e. fear, anger, hate, or jealousy). If you are looking at a picture of your favorite car and secretly feel jealous or angry because your friend bought one before you, you are way off track and are delaying the physical manifestation of your own desire. In the presence of any negative thoughts, your visualization work will be counter-productive if not self-sabotaging. In this case, I suggest you do some internal house-keeping first and eradicate any emotional skeletons. Only then will you be ready and able to steer your mind effectively and start hitting your objectives. On a final note, any images, feelings or thoughts that evoke one of the fourteen most extreme emotions have the strongest 'attractor factor', meaning creative force to manifest their corresponding vibration in a physical form (Vitale).

Your take-away: Only feed your mind with images that correspond to that, which you seek to experience in your life. Leverage this technique and first design your dream life visually. Choose every image with the outmost care because as David Cameron Gikandi reminds us:

"LIFE IS IMAGES OF THE MIND EXPRESSED"!

**

Specifically, life is images of YOUR mind expressed. To change your life, start changing images of your mind and start designing more exciting movie sets and more exhilarating movie scenes. Let me remind you that you have complete creative control. Whether you are aware of it or not, every time you sit down to watch TV, you become an ideal target of outside media programming and lose control over the nature of messages and images that reach your subconscious. The more conscious you become of this fact, the easier it will be for you to make the right conscious choices and thus start consciously co-creating your everyday life. Now ask yourself honestly: What are the current predominant images stored in your mind? What mental images take up the most of your 'mental hard-drive' at this very moment? If you are at home, close your eyes and see what images pop up.

As a final point on this topic, your mind responds to repetition and repetitive suggestions from self and the external environment (i.e. others, media, culture). Spiritual-preneurs censor their exposure to media programming and carefully select what messages they expose their minds to. Moreover, they cultivate another important success habit: positive auto-suggestion. Claude Bristol makes a useful observation on this topic:

"It is the power of suggestion that starts the machinery into operation or causes the subconscious mind to begin its creative work, and right here is where affirmations and repetitions play their part. It's the repetition [...] of the same affirmations that leads to belief, and once that belief becomes a deep conviction, things begin to happen".

***

Don't Just Team-Build but also Dream-Build

Let me ask you another important question that no one may have asked you before. What is the size of your dream? Can you see it? Can you somehow measure it? Can you feel it? Do you spend time with your dream? Do you take active steps to expand your dreams on a regular basis? Active dream-building is another success tool and an acquired success habit of accomplished spiritual-preneurs. They recognize the utmost importance of thinking and dreaming big, or at least dreaming bigger than most. Their ability and habit of thinking and dreaming big is what allows them to transcend the average and dismantle any self-imposed limits. If you are not familiar with Dr. David J. Schwartz's book titled the *Magic of Thinking Big*, I recommend that you add this classic to your library. The book sold over 6 million copies since its first publication in 1959.

And why all the fuss about thinking and dreaming big? It is the size of your dreams, the boldness of your thoughts (ideas), and your ability to think creatively that are instrumental in shaping your real-life experience. As Dr. Schwartz argues:

"You don't need to be an intellectual or have innate talent to attain great success and satisfaction - but you do need to learn and understand the habit of thinking and behaving in ways that will get you there".

This includes the habit of dreaming big. Let me share an experience. I was attending a 'dream weekend' rally, a Tony Robbins-type of event, when an MC of the three-day conference comes on stage to introduce the next speaker and begins like this:

"Good morning ladies and gentlemen. Let me start by saying that you should have a dream so big that it will take anywhere from 3 to 10 lifetimes to accomplish"!

**

The introduction intrigued me, yet I also found it strange. I do get the importance of dreaming big but dreams that take 10 lifetimes to accomplish? Several years later, this very same concept is not so odd to me anymore. If you want to live a life of success, fulfillment and happiness, you also have to play the role of a visionary and dream out all the possibilities. It is not always about the best strategy and the most effective team-building. Dreaming and thinking big and creatively is an essential success skill that all spiritual-preneurs nurture. If you are still not convinced, ask yourself this: "How much good can a high-performing team do in the absence of an inspiring dream that propels the team members forward? There are many other benefits of thinking and dreaming big. The act of expanding your dreams engages your imagination and creative mind and becomes the driving force for personal development. The bigger you dream and the bolder your thoughts, the bolder your action and the more powerful and stronger you grow as a result of this combination and your efforts.

It goes without saying that your goals - unlike your dreams - have to be believable and SMART (specific, measurable, attainable, realistic and timely). As Dr. Joe Vitale adds, they have to excite you, but also scare you a little so that you feel motivated to act on them. But be careful in defining your ambitions. If your goals are set too high, if they represent too big of a leap mentally or seem overwhelming instead of empowering, they run the risk of discouraging you and potentially stalling your conscious efforts. As far as your dreams go, there are no limits, so dream big and dream away!

Bottom line: take the time to re-discover your creative imagination, expansive thinking and dream-building that you may have exhibited as a child but later suppressed. Even as adults, we can all use a bit more playfulness in our day-to-day lives. Zig Ziglar concludes to this end:

"Without a question, human imagination or visualization and concentration are chief factors in developing the subconscious mind"!

Let me share one more useful tip. Your visualization efforts will be more effective if you make them as real as possible and involve all five senses. Do you recall our conversation about your mind not being able to tell the difference between a real scenario and an imagined one?

Let's suppose that you have your eyes set on new car and you have your image ready, you even photoshopped yourself into it. Now go test drive it! This very act will give you an opportunity to involve all your senses and will make any subsequent visualization efforts more effective. During the test-drive experience, you'll be able to feel and smell the leather interior, put your hands on the steering wheel, enjoy the new car smell and or the wind gently blowing in your face as you cruise along in this latest convertible model, your nose picking up exotic local smells of your favorite neighborhood. The more vivid the details of your experience, the more effective and magnetic your visualization work will be. While the exercise may sound a bit tedious at first, if you are going after the right things in life, all of this should be fun!

Now let me give you one more tip on how you can apply visualization beyond dream-building. Many golfers or athletes, for instance, perfect their real-life moves through mental and visual rehearsals. Once they have perfected their skill on the mental playing field, they will have also enhanced their ability to deliver the perfect swing on the real golf-course, to give an example. Take a good note of this mental skill-building tactic, as it can be applied to any under-taking. Pick a skill that you want to develop and then rehearse it in your mind to speed up its mastery.

To wrap up our topic at hand, your current life situation is a reflection of your dominant mental images and principal inner states (i.e. happiness or sadness). To change your life, change the images of your mind. You also have to be internally and energetically aligned, but we will get to this point.

But first, let me check-in with you quickly. Are you starting to feel a desire to change something about your life? Do you feel a subtle nudge to expand your goals or try one of the techniques discussed? If you are nodding and indicating a subtle 'yes', then this book is accomplishing its intended objective and the author is happy! Let's now carry on in our discussion of other spiritually-inspired strategies.

***

Wealth Creation Ritual: Visualized Meditation

As noted above, spiritual-preneurs have made playful visualization a regular wealth-building routine. They also resort to another effective success-building tool, which is visualized meditation. Mediation as a technique is both grounding and expansive in that it first quiets the mind, grounds and energetically recalibrates. The expansive component comes in the form of goal-setting and dream-building that accompanies it. The goal in a visualized meditation exercise is to keep expanding an already dynamic list of your dreams, goals and intentions and then turning them into their visual representations.

Here is a brief description of a customized meditation routine that is easy to follow. To start, set about 15-20 minutes aside at a time that is most convenient to you. Early mornings or late evenings are always suitable time slots. Induce a meditative atmosphere by listening to some ambient music or subliminal audios. Subliminal recordings are instrumental music with embedded non-verbal messages for your subconscious. This type of music quiets your racing mind and puts you in a relaxed and slightly hypnotic state, therefore increasing your overall receptivity. If you are interested, go on YouTube and type in subliminal music in the search menu. You will see there is no shortage of resources. You can choose specifically targeted music (i.e. abundance mindset). I am sure you will find something that is personally soothing.

Why are subliminal recordings or suggestions effective? Their encoded messages aimed at your subconscious are meant to clear any contradictory internal beliefs that may be holding you in certain undesirable patterns. I have personally witnessed tangible benefits. Aside from their energetic healing effect, I find subliminal audios calming in that they quiet my over-active conscious mind and put me in a more creative and highly productive state. See for yourself! I strongly recommend adding some of these audios to your e-library, especially if you feel that you have not making the kind of progress that you would like to see. They can be a real transformation catalyst, remove any hidden blocks or light fire where it needs to be lit. Furthermore, scientific research shows that subliminal recordings are most effective when combined with repetitive suggestions of empowering creative imagery (pictures). To carry on with your meditation exercise, select your goal (chief aim), get its visual representation, and as you listen to the subliminal music, play out various desired scenarios related to your goal in the theatre of your own mind. Feel content and happy about having already achieved. Imagine yourself celebrating with your groups of friends and family, knowing that there are many more successes and celebrations to come! This is what you can expect at the end of your meditation exercise:

Your Goal - Corresponding Image - Positive Emotion - Repetitive Suggestion - Harmonizing Music to engage other senses = CREATIVE INSPIRATION!

Every time you feel inspired, write a new empowering script for yet another episode of your *Incredible Life* movie. If you approach building this habit from this playful stance, it will be more fun, and your conscious mind will not interfere.

The more vivid and real you make your script-writing and movie-directing work, the more reflective and rewarding your real-life situations and outcomes will be. Think about this: how many of us spend hours and hours glued to the TV, living someone else's life for weeks at a time through reality-TV shows? Why not spend some of that time on your own movie set, developing and scripting your own life legacy film? The more you engage in this practice of scripting and visualizing in the context of a meditative atmosphere, the more your real-life circumstance will start resembling the life your created in your fictional movie. And then you realize that the line between your movie script and your life has suddenly blurred. You are living a blissful, happy and abundant existence! You have arrived! Or, as the popular lifestyle magazine Robb Report headlines, you are living "LUXURY without COMPROMISE"!

Last but not least, a personal anecdote on the creative power of emotionalized imagery and repetitive suggestion to address any lingering disbelief. Back in 2014, I cut out a clipping from a cruise-line marketing brochure that happened to outline an itinerary around the Adriatic Sea, leaving from the Port of Venice. I strategically put the picture on my dream-board above the stove. Since I love to cook, I knew that I'd get to look at the image every time I'd be preparing a meal so that spot was definitely strategically convenient. One year later, my brother was getting married in the High Tatra mountains in Slovakia and so a trip to Europe was on the agenda that year. As we were planning the wedding, we found an unbelievably discounted cruise around the Adriatic that we were not initially planning on taking. Before I even had a chance to analyze, were leaving for a week-long cruise out of the port of Venice. Only as the ship sailed off into the sunset did I realize that the itinerary we were about to do hit pretty much 6 out of 7 ports that were hanging on my dream-board for about a year. Let me remind you that I did not focus on this particular image that intently or study the itinerary too closely. It was the power of the repetitive suggestion that made my subconscious mind take notice and subsequently helped orchestrate this lovely European vacation. Can you believe that we even ended up on the cruise-line's in-room TV channel providing a testimonial about our wonderful Adriatic experience? We certainly made a lot of cruise friends that year!

Command Your Built-in Success Mechanism

Let me ask you another question: what do successful spiritual-preneurs do when they accomplish their goal? What do they when they realize their biggest dream that they were so intently after? And what would you do in that instance? Make this question real, think of that one big dream that you have and ask yourself: "What am I going to do when this dream becomes my reality"? Are you going to kick back and relax, perhaps retire, or are you going to focus on something new? Spiritual-preneurs realize the importance of continuously expanding their goals and establishing new and more challenging ones. While success is a journey, they know that they are never quite done arriving. They know that it would take them at least a few lifetimes to realize their full potential. They know that there is always room to make a greater impact, stretch more and go beyond what one thought possible.

A common mistake that many of us make is that we fail to replace our accomplished goal with a new one; a goal that is even more ambitious, more daring or bolder. I advise that you follow in the footsteps of other spiritual-preneurs, who are aware that their internal machinery always needs a meaningful focal point. And when you get to the finish line, make sure that you have your next goal already lined up. What happens if you don't? In the absence of a goal, your attention and focus turn from pursuing your worthy goal to protecting that, which you have achieved. If you do not assign yourself a new purpose (goal) and refocus your efforts on the pursuit of another constructive endeavor, your attention will be drawn to protecting that, which you had already achieved and are in possession of (i.e. financial goal, reputation, relationships). An over-protective stance eventually transforms into fear of losing and the inevitable loss follows. The take-away is that the only way to live a successful and satisfying life is to be constantly pursuing new, bigger, better, more ambitious, bolder goals and more inspiring dreams. Continuous growth, forward movement and dynamic creation is the spiritual-MBA way! As Albert Einstein further comments:

"Life is like riding a bicycle. To keep your balance, you have to move forward".

**

Let's now re-direct our attention and spend a few minutes talking about this built-in success mechanism that we are all equipped with and that is strictly goal-driven. What the New Thought proponents call genie-of-the-mind, life principle, or 'mind power', the scientific community calls an 'automatic servo-mechanism' or a 'built-in guidance system' (Dr. Maltz, *The New Psycho-Cybernetics*). The noun 'servo' means "to serve" and indicates that this mechanism needs to be consistently fed new goals, as it is programmed for forward movement. If properly managed and commanded, this powerful mechanism allows you to literally "engineer the personality and the life that you desire" (Maltz). The principles of psycho-cybernetics have changed lives of over 30 million people. The name of the discipline itself is a derived from a Greek word that means "the steersman", which suggests that you and only you are the steersman (or steerswoman) of this precious system. In brief, the field of psycho-cybernetics teaches "how to effectively communicate with and through the self-image so as to better control the servo-mechanism within" (Maltz). This includes the development of a positive mindset, positive self-talk and visualization of success. To succeed, hold an image of yourself as someone who is important, significant, influential, and as someone who wins and succeeds at every undertaking. There are no limits when it comes to redefining your vision and image of self!

But let's now digress for a moment to give you some context: Dr. Maxwell Maltz was a renowned American cosmetic surgeon who got interested in examining the link between life success and one's self-image. He became particularly interested in understanding this link, when he saw his own patients turn their lives around, and this was after he successfully corrected their physical deformities through plastic surgery. After several years of practice, he observed that his patients' lives always significantly improved post-surgery. He studied the link and proposed that such outcomes were plausible due to the fact that surgical corrections of physical deformities were followed by corrections of his patients' perceived self-image. Otherwise put, when their physical scars disappeared, Dr. Maltz's patients were finally free to remove their deep emotional scars that were eating away at their self-image. Once these scars were removed surgically, Dr. Maltz's patients were able to clear their self-imposed limits. They were then ready and able to achieve any level of success and happiness that they desired. Dr. Maltz observations and clinical experiences led him to become an expert in the field of psycho-cybernetics. He goes on to describe that:

"Every living thing has a built-in guidance system or goal-striving device, put there by the Creator to help achieve its goal – which is, in broad terms to live. This guidance system steers you in the right direction […] and also serves as an ELECTRONIC BRAIN which can function automatically to solve problems, give you needed answers, and provide new ideas and inspirations".

**

Here is a quick reminder to help you better manage your electronic brain so to speak. Once you have identified your goal and communicated it effectively to your internal machinery, you have to detach from the final outcome. This circles back to our recent discussion of the *Law of Detachment*. As Dr. Maltz observes on the subject:

"Once the decision is reached and execution is in order of the day, dismiss absolutely all responsibility and care about the outcome. Unclamp the intellectual and practical machinery and let it run free"!

Bottom line: That different communities of experts, from spiritual gurus to scientists and medical professionals, keep arriving at converging conclusions about the nature and detailed functioning of our internal software even further underscores the validity of this material. I trust that you are finding it to be of value.

***

Your Emotional Guidance System

Aside from the automatic goal-striving mechanism, your human engineering also comes with an emotional guidance system. Call it your internal frequency barometer. Spiritual-preneurs use this internal indicator to read the quality of their thoughts. They know that if feel good, their thoughts are positive. This is because positive and negative cannot occupy your mind at the same time. Said differently, it is impossible to feel good and think negative thoughts at the same time (Byrne). Let's test it out! Have you ever thought about a luxurious vacation in Cartagena, Singapore or Panama City and felt infuriated upon the thought of you enjoying the white sandy beach and soaking in the tropical sun? Impossible! In this sense, your feelings are an accurate barometer of your overall vibrational pull and its relative direction. The more extreme the emotion, the stronger your creative power and its 'attractor factor', as we have seen. Put simply, your emotions tell you if you are creating in the positive or working out of the negative and self-sabotaging. It may be therefore to your benefit to start monitoring your emotions more consciously, so that you learn how to read your internal guidance system quickly and accurately. You also need to know when you need to make an energetic switch, which simply means changing your activity to raise your frequency. You do this by simply turning to an activity that makes you feel good.

To sum it up, when you feel good, you know your thoughts are positive and success-supporting and you are on the right track. The minute you detect a negative feeling, your thoughts have become contaminated and could signal a case of internal misalignment, which we will talk about. When negative thoughts and emotions hijack your being, you need to do something to self-correct rather than remain in a state of feeling angry, sad or depressed etc. You need to refocus and change up your activity. Sing, dance, talk to a cheerful person, go to a park, play with a pet, paint, exercise or choose anything else that does the trick. The habit of feeling good along with your ability to read and manage your emotions quickly effectively are both critical tools of your spiritual-MBA toolkit.

To end with a practical tip, one of the fastest ways to self-correct and raise your vibration is by practicing gratitude. Next time you get angry or sad, stop what you are doing at that moment and write down 3 things that have in your life and are grateful for. You can also think about your past accomplishments or reminisce about a deeply cherished childhood memory. The latter always does the trick for me. Or you can also start cleaning, and by that I do not mean physically cleaning your house. Keep on reading to find out what kind of cleaning I am referring to! Now allow me to conclude this section on mind management by introducing you to two fun wealth-consciousness building games. Both of them were designed to raise your vibration, engage your imagination, visualization skills and help you expand your dream-list or what I call your prosperity list.

***

The Prosperity Game: Step into The Flow

In 2004, New York Times best-selling author Esther and Jerry Hicks published a best-selling book of teachings of a non-physical entity Abraham titled *Ask and It Is Given. Learning How to Manifest Your Desires*. This is what Louise L. Hay, the founder of Hay

House publishing, motivational speaker and New Thought author remarked about this publication:

> "**One of the most valuable things about "*Ask and It is Given*" is that Abraham gives us 22 powerful processes to achieve our goals. No matter where we are, there is a process that can make our lives better**".

**

The prosperity game is adapted from Esther and Jerry Hick's best-seller. It is a fun, creative process that expands your dream-building and goal-setting ability. But the main benefit of the game is that it can enhance the flow of money and abundance into your life. Requirements for the game: pen, paper, plenty of imagination, and access to Google. Here are the 'rules of engagement'. Your first step: set a start date and designate it as Day 1. On this day, you have $1000 deposited in your imaginary checking account or on your imaginary credit card. Now here is where the game gets interesting. On Day 2, your credit account is showing a deposit of $2,000, or $1000 more than the previous day. Day 3 shows a deposit of $3,000, Day 4 shows $4,000 and so forth. If you play this game for one year (365 days), you will have allocated and spent over $66,000,000=\$66$ Million dollars. The game clearly also tests your commitment and perseverance or the C+3P formula of success.

The daily allocation of money in this game is yours to spend any way you want, as long as your choices are supporting your dream life and the realization of your potential. You do have a few choices to make along the way. You can spend your daily allocation at once, or you can accumulate your capital to make a bigger purchase later. Since your objective here is to exercise your imagination, spending all of your money on one or two large items will defeat the purpose of this creative process. Your primary objective in this game is to expand your imagination and build on an existing list of dreams, goals, and intentions. You already know that dollars come to those who know what to do with the abundance, so think big and creatively as you are making your financial allocations and imaginary purchases. Money comes to those who know how to best deploy it. To this point, Dr. Joe Vitale reminds you that:

"Money is like an empty vessel, waiting to be filled with your passions, intuitions and missions"!

When it comes to the prosperity game, Esther and Jerry Hicks state that it is also a powerful tool "for shifting your vibrational point of attraction". This is because "the universe makes no distinction between the vibration you offer in response to what you are living and the vibration you offer in response to what you are imaging", which in this case happens in the form of your fictional purchases. You can see how this game then reinforces your wealth mentality and turns you into a more powerful money (success) magnet.

Let your imagination go wild and keep building a 'running list' of everything you wish to experience, be, do, know and have in life. The prosperity game inspired me to extend my own list of desires and dreams and lead me to start a Vision8888 project. This is simply a dream-list with a total of 8888 items across various categories that I am still collecting. Some of these include new skills and performance goals, new experiences, travel, financial and real-estate investments, philanthropy, business goals, international joint venture projects, spiritual wealth, hobbies, art, and the list goes on and on. The key point is to have fun and feel good as you are systematically building it and thinking about it.

Your Three Musketeers: Manage This Trio

Spiritual-preneurs follow a strict daily routine that plentifully nourishes and stimulates their mind, body and soul. If you wish to lead a happy and healthy life, I recommend you do the same. Here are some proven tips from various experts and other entrepreneurs. Your first responsibility is to look after your physical vessel (temple) that is your body. Treat it with the outmost care, as healthy body is a sure sign of a healthy self-image, self-respect and self-love. It is also your foundation for lasting wealth and happiness, as nothing can be achieved without optimal health. As Sharon Anne Klinger and Sandra Anne Taylor comment:

"It is only when you treat yourself better that you declare to the Universe that you deserve better"!

Moreover, your healthy body is an indication that you have mastered two other key success principles and that is self-control and self-discipline. This is clearly not the case if you are 50 pounds overweight.

On the subject of nutrition, the most common reason for not eating well is a lack of knowledge or time to prepare a healthy meal. One of the most effective and easy-to-follow nutritional plans that I came to know and tested over the years is the fast metabolism plan designed by Ms. Haylie Pomroy. Haylie is a nutritionist based in Los Angeles, California. You can learn more about the principles behind her nutritional system that became massively popular at www.fastmetabolismdiet.com. If you feel that your body is not functioning properly, you may benefit from this 28-day program that also serves as a full-body cleanse. The program is easy to follow even if you are travelling and you can also easily extend it past the 28 days and follow it on an ongoing basis. My family has been eating in line with the principles of the fast metabolism diet for almost 4 years and I personally have never felt more vibrant, energetic and clear-minded. And the real bonus for me personally? I managed to maintain optimal health and proper eating habits despite all the travelling!

There is one more rather spiritual benefit to keeping your body healthy and toxin-free. A clean and well-functioning body gives you clarity of mind and facilitates your communication with your intuitive or higher Self. Put simply, keeping healthy and in tune with your body allows you to hear your intuitive nudges and universal whispers. The topic of energetic healing is coming up in the next segment.

To close off our discussion of body and health management, I recommend daily walks, yoga, and regular cardio if possible. I am also a big believer in a regular trampoline rebounding and the benefits of laughing. In case you didn't know, it has been proven that laughing lowers your blood pressure, improves cardiac health and triggers the release of endorphins. It also works your abs, as does trampoline rebounding. Bouncing on a trampoline for about 4 min helps drain your lymphatic system of accumulated toxins. And why 4 minutes? That is exactly how long it takes for your lymphatic fluid to circulate throughout your body once. One 4-minute circuit is all you need to filter out some of the impurities. For an increased benefit, double up the time.

NOURISH YOUR MIND: LEADERS ARE READERS

Spiritual-preneurs, like other self-aware leaders, exercise and train their mind through an established self-development routine. They read a variety of inspirational and self-development material for at least an hour a day, ideally first thing in the morning or before going to bed. What's unique about these two specific times? According to the scientific community, this is when your mind is most malleable, suggestible and susceptible to external impressions and auto-suggestions. Reserve these times for some meaningful inner work if you can. If a long-commute is your daily reality, use the time in transit to listen to some mind-stimulating podcasts and or self-development audios. Be creative and turn your idle time into a mobile university! Every moment gives you a new opportunity to make the right choice; a new choice that either keeps you where you are or helps you advance and thus serves your higher purpose.

EMOTIONAL BALANCE & SELF-CONTROL

Another key success habit of spiritual-preneurs is their emotional balance, steadiness and self-control. Put simply, nothing throws them off easily because and they have learned how to control their responses to situations, people, events or circumstances. You may not like to hear it but your degree of self-control partly determines how far you get in life. It is not what happens, but how you respond to what happens that matters the most and has the greatest impact on the end-result. As Tony Robbins claims, it is now what happens, but the meaning that you assign to what happens and your response to the event that is your most critical success factor. In short, your responses can turn even the best possible situation, relationship or an event into a nightmare. And vice versa, even the most disastrous of situations has in it a seed of an equivalent advantage, if only your attitude and emotional response allows you to see it. If you still get upset at times, don't beat yourself up but forgive. Remind yourself, as Deepak Chopra reminds us, that when you get angry and lose your cool, you have lost control over a part of Self and have gone unconscious. Then self-correct!

ON THE SUBJECT of SPIRIT: ENERGETIC HOUSE-KEEPING

In addition to keeping their bodies healthy and toxin-free and their minds engaged and stimulated, spiritual-preneurs also maintain their energetic field clean and metaphorically unobstructed. This of course requires some intuitive inner work, rebalancing, reflection, stillness, silenced meditation, including some energetic healing to delete any energetic debris. Why is this clearing work so important? If you do not take your emotional garbage out on a regular basis, it will metamorphose into some form of internal resistance. This may start off small at first, but will eventually grow if not dealt with, delaying or ultimately sabotaging your progress. How to overcome internal resistance and clean your body energetically is our next topic.

The energetic techniques that I am about to introduce had a real transformational effect on several spiritual entrepreneurs that I know. A regular use of these techniques led them to greater personal performance, greater opportunities and an increased excitement for life. Once they started attending to their energetic bodies, dealt with their inner hang-ups and realigned, they started to experience greater happiness and abundance on all fronts. I will explain what this all means as we go along. Obviously, these spiritual-preneurs consistently worked all of the other tools of their spiritual self-leadership toolkit.

Your first step, like with anything, is to identify what type of resistance you might be dealing with. It is ok, if not necessary, to take time with this process that involves some delicate inner work. Many of us live in a state of denial or limited self-awareness and may be slow to see, or even resistant to admit, what's standing in our way. Rest assured, most of us have some lingering issues from the past that we have been running away from, instead of resolving them once and for all. Over time, these suppressed past issues may have grown into emotional monsters and are now creating some major internal resistance. If this topic resonates at some level, you have to do some honest self-inquiry and introspective work and then deal with the unwanted, clearing any outstanding issues one by one. It takes some time, but you are the only one, who can make a serious commitment to this much needed internal house-keeping. You have to clear the way in order to succeed!

Before we proceed, let me point out some obvious signs that are indicative of cases of internal resistance. 1) you keep missing your goals and are not seeing tangible results despite you taking appropriate action 2) you keep feeling hopeless and victimized 3) you do not see any steps that you can take at the moment to move forward; 4) you feel stuck and procrastinate.

As you may know, your internal house-keeping work starts with cultivating a solid relationship with yourself, especially if there is a reason to believe that you still do not have a solid one. In fact, psychologists believe that the quality of your relationships with others is a reflection of the kind of relationship that you have with yourself. Interestingly, this relationship is founded on your relationship with your inner Self. So how can you asses the strength and quality of your own self-love? There is a simple and intuitive way. Answer this question: are you comfortable spending an entire day or two with yourself, completely alone, no TV, limited phone, maybe some music but no interaction with others, not even your partner? A complete solitude for at least a day! If the answer is no, then ask yourself if you are looking for distractions because you are running away from something that you should have dealt with a long time ago. Are you avoiding your own self, an overdue internal issue, reconciling a broken promise? Only you know what that might be. And if you do not know, start the process of an honest self-inquiry, engaging the help of your intuitive Self. That is, if you are you able to hear and willing to listen to the messages that come to you from a higher perspective.

***

Can You Hear Your Spiritual Self?

Let me share one more secret. Your ability to hear messages from your inner Self and your ability to communicate with your internal mechanisms is another pre-requisite for creating and living the life of your dreams! Interestingly, you will greatly enhance your 'spiritual communication skills' if you integrate meditation into your daily practice. Meditation as a popular spiritual practice that enables you to shut off your busy logical and analytical mind and thus creates an opportunity to go within. An opportunity to be still. Turning within means going to the source or your life instinct, your Spiritual Self, that is in turn connected to the universal intelligence.

Spiritual-preneurs devote regular time to the practice and refinement of their ability to communicate with their higher Self. If you are open-minded enough and prefer a more playful approach, I suggest integrating additional tools to guide your communication with the spiritual realm, such as some of Doreen Virtue's materials. While Doreen recently shifted the direction of her work, she is a world-known intuitive healer, author, motivational speaker and an authority on communicating with the spiritual dimension. Doreen's home-base is in Hawaii. Her most known publications are on the subject of cosmic language, numerology and angel numbers. She has written extensively on the spiritual realm and its communication with our physical three-dimensional world. If the goal of your meditations is to enhance your communication with your spiritual Self, reach for some of Doreen's practical tools, such as the angel therapy oracle cards or other tarot card sets. I was personally surprised at the consistency of messages that these tools would deliver.

I hear you and I am well aware that the idea of working with tarot cards may seem out of place for some. However, the spiritual dimension is as real as our physical world so why not reach for any available tools that may make our communication more focused and effective? Working with spiritually-inspired tools such as the tarot has its benefits; it has the potential to deliver new insights about Self, your journey, life purpose or new unforeseen opportunities or potential roadblocks. Personally, spiritual readings provided me with some fresh insights that guided me to some invaluable discoveries. I am happy to have tapped into the wisdom of this realm and my spiritual Self. As another intuitive healer and spiritual teacher Selacia claims:

> **"The higher (spiritual) view is not linear, but it factors in the eternal quantum Self and larger quantum reality".**

***

GETTING TO ZERO

Now let me ask you this. Have you been trying to catch this inner whisper but cannot hear a thing? If this is the case, it may be a sign that you are in need of some energetic clearing or a 'repair' of a potential internal misalignment. As an example, you are internally misaligned when your conscious thoughts are focused on success and visualize a successful achievement of a certain goal, but your inner feelings are in a direct contradiction. Instead of self-efficacy and enthusiasm, you are vibrating doubt, uncertainty and fear. It is critical for you to realize that this internal misalignment shows up in your life as a counter-intentions (Vitale). As the word suggests, counter-intentions are counter-productive and can potentially sabotage the realization of your dreams and goals.

Counter-intentions are a common form of resistance and due to their destructive nature have to be cleared out. This starts with identifying them, which is not always an easy task, as your energetic clutter wears different masks. One such mask comes in the form of unresolved past memories. Ask yourself! Is there a past memory or an incident that you have not fully processed and keep carrying around? Is there an issue that keeps resurfacing in your life and every time it does, you push it further inside? If the answer is yes, keep on reading as you are about to discover a quick and easy clearing technique.

When any lingering negative memories are cleared, you arrive at "zero". This concept was coined by Dr. Ihaleakala Hew Len, a famous Hawaiian psychologist, author and a spiritual teacher. Dr. Hew Len goes on to explain that when you are at 'zero', you are clear of all past negative memories and any other energetic attachments that may span across generations. This is what he calls 'ancestral memories', which are the culprit in some instances. When all of your energetic debris and past ancestral attachments are cleared, your spiritual senses, including your spiritual sight and ability to hear your inner self, will improve in noticeable ways. You will then be ready and able to hear and interpret any intuitive messages that the universe is sending you. As a secondary bonus of getting clear, the Divine inspiration starts to flow through you and you feel daily excitement and exhilaration. You feel that you have arrived because you can hear your Self!

On a final point, when you get clear, you do not procrastinate. You take inspired action and quickly slip into the success momentum. Let me now give you the recipe. It is my hope that by the time you are through with these pages, you will see how critical 'getting clear' is. It is another required step that spiritual-preneurs take, as it leads to more joyful and successful life experience. For those who seek to create substantial financial wealth, getting clear and vibrationally aligned is not only essential, but also required in order to get into the universal flow prosperity and stay in it.

While formal education and world at large still values logic over intuition, successful spiritual-preneurs became successful because they tapped into their inner reservoir of power and allowed themselves to be partly guided by their inner Self. Now let's move along in our discussion of energetic work and discuss some specific tools found in the spiritual-MBA toolkit.

***

Overcoming Resistance & Allowing

Who's your favorite Hollywood celebrity or someone that you adore and want to trade your life with, even if you've never told anyone? Think of that person and imagine their life clearly. If you did trade your life with this idol of yours for a day or two, you would quickly realize that no irrespective of your celebrity or wealth status, each of us have our own set of challenges, obstacles or personal dramas which serve as our learning opportunities. Our decision, commitment and determination in overcoming these obstacles is at the very core of our life journey toward self-realization, happiness and success. In fact, the only thing that separates any self-made successes from the masses is their sheer drive, discipline and determination to overcome whatever challenges life threw on their path. These folks are in essence just like you and me, but they are no longer standing in their own way. They are no longer disconnected from their true Self, they are in their self-power and aware of the limitless power or the life principle that runs through them and the universe.

If you are not attracting the right set of circumstances, if you are in a rut, or if your progress is minimal despite great efforts taken, then read on and listen carefully. The goal of the next section is twofold: 1) to make you aware of what could be holding you back, whether it is your limiting beliefs, past memories, fears, lack of self-confidence etc. Secondly 2), to add a few energetic healing tools to an already robust self-leadership toolkit. These techniques can be applied at your own leisure and have the potential to clear any lingering limiting beliefs, negative thoughts and emotions and other mental blocks that may be causing your stagnation or under-performance.

Limiting Beliefs: What You Need to Know

"It is not what you eat, but what you digest that makes you stronger.

It is not what you earn, but what you retain that builds your wealth.

It is not what you learn, but what you remember that makes you wise".

The above quote comes from personal notes taken at a motivational event attended back in 2012 in San Diego, California. What's the underlying message? If you are still not living the life of your dreams despite all your diligent work; if you are experiencing difficulty staying motivated and following through on your goals; if you are a logic-driven person who is numb to the intuitive side; if you keep eating, but cannot digest, keep learning but cannot remember and keep earning but cannot retain, you have some more internal clearing and alignment work to do! This simply means that you may be still holding on to some limiting beliefs about yourself, about your life or the world at large. More often than not, we also hold inaccurate beliefs about our ability to succeed. Our distorted views and perceptions often lead us to assign an inaccurate meaning to events and situations that we go through, and this distorts our overall life experience or at least our perception of it and our subsequent actions and responses.

As the science of psychology has shown, all of your limiting beliefs and fears are lodged in your subconscious. This creates almost an instant conflict between beliefs entertained between your two minds: your conscious and subconscious one. Unless this conflict is reconciled, you will hold yourself in a perpetual cycle of stagnation and potential self-sabotage. For instance, if you are a hypochondriac or simply do not view yourself as a healthy person, do not expect to find it in your real-life experience. Here is another example. You are one of the highest performing Directors in your department. Your career goal for this year is to get that upcoming VP position at your current firm. This is your conscious decision and a logical, rational conclusion that you had make. You have been with the firm for over seven years, your last performance review was stellar and there is no one else more qualified for this internal promotion. Do you stand a chance? It depends! This hypothetical scenario is a good illustration of the topic at hand.

The problem is, your subconscious mind holds a contradictory view of what you are capable of or what you deserve because of a belief that was formed based on an incident that happened a few decades ago. In other words, you internalized a past issue but hadn't dealt with. Your subconscious mind is now receiving counter-intentions that are a direct result of your outdated belief. Rest assured that once your current beliefs are accurately updated, any limiting views about self will be cleared, and you will then be 'in the clear' to move ahead! These counter-programs, that many of us run in our mental backdrop, are directly responsible for the delayed manifestations of our goals and dreams. Did you know that? This happens for one simple reason: your subconscious programming carries with it a stronger creative courant that overrides whatever message or decisions your rational mind makes.

There is one more danger. Your outdated views and counter-intentions can prevent your affirmative messages related to the achievement of your goals from getting through to your subconscious. Among other things, spiritual-preneurs use hypnosis to clear any internal jams or internal communication glitches. As a matter of fact, studies have shown hypnosis to be an effective technique that clears self-sabotaging cellular memory lodged in your subconscious. Hypnosis is defined as a "state of human consciousness involving focused attention, reduced peripheral awareness and enhanced capacity to respond to suggestion" (Wikipedia). It is another tool of your self-leadership toolkit and one of the best ways to re-program and re-align your subconscious and conscious minds and recalibrate your inner programing for success.

**

If you keep experiencing what I call 'near-misses' in life, chances are that you are hanging on to an element from the past. This could be an outdated belief that originated in a context that was personally relevant several decades ago (i.e. school context) but that is still the driving force of your counter-intentions. Why are these counter-programs so detrimental to your success and happiness? They prevent you from getting into a vibrational harmony (alignment) with that which you wish to create and experience.

For the sake of clarity, a near-miss means that you are always one step away from hitting your goal, but you are never quite there. In other words, you keep experiencing close calls. You almost closed on a sale as a realtor, almost aced that job interview, and almost got accepted to the school of your first choice. While you may be intently focused on and taking aggressive action to accomplish your goals, your inner world may be screaming disbelief, doubt, fear, lack of self-love, guilt etc. How can you expect to experience happiness or any other positive outcome if your inner world is sending out messages that are diametrically opposed?

The question is, why do we hold on to these outdated beliefs instead of altering them so that they more accurately reflect our current beliefs and realities? We do so for one simple reason. Because we do not know any better and are not aware of their insidious nature. How can we question or challenge something that we do not even know exists? Instead of examining and upgrading our limiting views, we often end up reinforcing them and with that our unsatisfying existence. Unless…something jolts us out of our comfort zone, awakens us and creates an opportunity for our self-awareness to expand. This could be an incident, an encounter, a circumstance, a book that you read! Bottom line: to live the life of boundless wealth and happiness that you deserve, you need to uncover any outdated beliefs or limiting patterns (thought or behavioral ones) that may be holding back. You then have to eradicate them one by one, the same way you take out any unwanted weeds in your own garden of abundance.

As my experiences revealed, some of the more stubborn issues and strongly reinforced destructive patterns have to be unraveled bit by bit, through a gentle yet effective spiritual technique of honest self-inquiry. For about four years now, I have been a regular reader of an online blog called the Spirit Library. The way this site came to me is quite serendipitous in itself, but that is not the point. I follow a shortlist of key contributors, most of whom are spiritual astrologers and intuitive healers. Selacia, whom I mentioned a few pages back, is one of them. Selacia is a globally known writer, DNA intuitive healer and a spiritual teacher. In one of her blogs, Selacia talked about questions to pose to your inner Self if your progress is hindered, if you are uncertain about the direction of your life path, or if you feel that something is missing in your life. Selacia encourages that you go within, get specific with your meditative inquiry and ask your spiritual Self the following:

"What is the main thing that I need to add, eliminate, or change, to have more success and joy? What learned coping mechanisms am I applying that

are now a hindrance and blocking my way forward"?

**

The "learned coping mechanisms" that Selacia talks about could be your outdated beliefs and old programs that are running in the background. These programs limit your thinking and compromise your actions and behaviors. You have to identify these limiting beliefs first, examine and understand, then replace with more accurate and constructive ones. This is where positive affirmations can serve as a useful tool. Please refer to Appendix C for an illustrative list.

BELIEFS IN DISGUISE

The main argument entertained here is that limiting beliefs are destructive and will hinder your happiness, success and achievement if not dealt with. As you now know, they show up as counter-programs, although it is sometimes difficult to establish a direct link. What do I mean? If you are living in a state of victimhood, your counter-program could be a negative self-talk such as this: "Nothing ever-works-out-for-me! Life is tough! There are no good opportunities!" If your limiting belief about Self is that you are not worthy or good enough, your counter-program will be behavioral self-sabotage.

Successful spiritual-preneurs are highly aware and take the necessary time to examine, challenge and upgrade their beliefs as they evolve, succeed, gather new experiences and expand their perspectives. I have to admit, growing up in the old Soviet-world did not do much good for the development of my wealth consciousness. Once I became aware of my own limiting view in this regard, I made a conscious choice to replace a scarcity-oriented mindset by thoughts of unlimited wealth and prosperity. When I finally woke up, I was able to see how the kind of thinking that got me to where I was, was not going to get me to where I wanted to go next. To this point, I am sharing with you one of my favorite affirmations that reinforces my prosperity consciousness.

"The more money I give and spend, the more money I get"!

Bottom line: If you want to expand and enrich your life, start examining and updating your beliefs (views). You are here to design the destiny that you seek, so make sure that your collective beliefs and behavioral patterns are supporting you on your journey.

And the bonus in this exercise? As you engage in this internal house-keeping and start clearing self-imposed limitations, you will be suddenly able to see new opportunities that your outdated views did not allow you to see or access before. Clear and replace what's no longer working for you and your life will be more fulfilling and intercepted with what seem to be magical moments that you would only dream about in the past. Remember, "life is images of your mind expressed" (Gikandi). Life is also a reflection of your inner programming that you may or may not be aware of. Maybe it is time to look inside!

***

Mind-Sync or Energetic Integrity

As you recall, your self-imposed limitations, such as doubts or fears, are housed in the darkest room of your subconscious. Once you have identified some limiting patters that have literally become your physical chains, you have to do some targeted repair work in your mental workshop. As Dr. Ted Morter, the founder of an energetic synchronization technique argues, "nothing happens in your physical body until it first appears in your energetic field". This goes back to the idea that your successes (or failures) are created in your mind first because "90% of your mental life is subconscious" (Dr. Morter).

Therefore, an essential part of your mind-management work is ensuring that both your conscious and subconscious minds are in sync. That they are congruent and energetically aligned, sending out mutually-reinforcing rather than contradictory messages. This is what some experts call achieving 'energetic or mind-integrity'. When you get to this point, you have cleared all limiting beliefs and counter-programs. But if your two minds are still in a disaccord, it will be your subconscious programming that wins, and you manifest in life whatever corresponds to its predominant energies. These energies are, in more cases than not, energies of fear, doubt, insecurities and everything else but a winning mindset. On a side note, the concept of mind-sync is not at all new. Back in his day, Napoleon Hill commented on the importance of internal or harmonious co-operation between your conscious and subconscious mind.

Spiritual-preneurs know that they are in full control when it comes to their internal machinery and have a few tools in their spiritual toolkit to manage any potential mind disharmony. They act as active steersmen (steerswoman) of their precious asset and take immediate measures to re-align, if they realize that their beliefs and actions are out of sync. On a personal note, one of my old programs that I replaced long-time ago was an outdated belief that I had to work twice as hard to accomplish something, not because I had to, but because working hard was a way to demonstrate extreme self-discipline.

So here comes another question. Where are you currently at: in a state of mind-sync or system's glitch? Take some time to examine your own internal programs that may be over-riding or undermining your conscious efforts. And when you finish your inner-world discovery trip and have found your internal glitch (program), you can start looking for its sponsoring thought or experience that keeps this program alive. As you can see, much of this work is internal but there are some effective techniques that will help you achieve the required energetic alignment.

***

The B.E.S.T. Technique

The bio-energetic synchronization technique, also known as the B.E.S.T. is one such tool. It was developed by Dr. Morter Jr., who describes it as "a non-forceful energy balancing technique that helps to re-establish the full healing potential of the body". It balances the body, mind, memory, and spirit energy fields, enhancing the flow of that energy throughout the entire system. The B.E.S.T. is a whole-body healing technique that synchronizes any short-circuited neurological patterns that linger due to unresolved emotional issues. In other words, any past traumas, incidents, experiences that have not been processed or dealt with properly will pollute your energetic bodies and dampen your ability to create and manifest. Dr. Popkin, a chiropractor and a practitioner of this energetic healing method comments on the subject:

"With B.E.S.T., the idea is to almost update all the information in your mind. After the timing has been knocked off by a trauma, all sorts of systems are out of sync, including structure, function, digestion and overall energy levels. With time, other issues surface and the body responds to past memories as opposed to what it is feeling at any given moment. This technique can reset the body and mind, just as the name suggests".

The synchronization or re-alignment work can serve as a real performance catalyst, as it eliminates any form of internal resistance and thus allows you to get unstuck and move forward. It is always refreshing to start with a clean slate, which is in this case a clean energetic body. As the above quote suggests, the untold secret lies in clearing not only limiting and short-circuited neurological patterns, but also any negative memories. This is a core belief of many ancient healing methods and practices. The reason your negative memories can hold you back is that they can cause a 'memory drag' that pulls you into the past and reactivates the memory that keeps you in an undesirable energetic pattern.

You become a victim of a memory drag when something external reactivates this past memory and you get unconsciously dragged into an old pattern attached to that past experience. Instead of responding to what is in front of you, a subconscious response pattern takes over and overrides your conscious programming. The past overtakes you, you lose your focus on the present and your state of unconsciousness dilutes your self-power. Spiritual-preneurs have resolved the unresolved. They released any destructive past memories and have forged a clear path forward! Now let me conclude this section by providing an everyday example of a memory drag and its end result.

Context: you are in your twenties. You have a bad first interview or a bad first date. Your second one is even worse, and you draw a faulty conclusion about self that in turn shapes your self-image. You conclude that you are bad at interviews or at interacting with people of the opposite sex. Since that day, every time you find yourself in a situation that is similar to that horrible interview or date, a memory gets triggered and you under-perform or self-sabotage. You lose control over Self and allow your past memory of that one bad experience to hijack your ability to perform and showcase your talents.

Can you see that this cycle has to be broken? You have to clear this memory and re-frame. Re-framing is a concept introduced by the famous motivational speaker and life coach Tony Robbins. As Tony teaches his followers, it is not what happens to us, but the meaning that we assign to what happens that is a critical success factor and can literally make us or break us. It is the difference between viewing anything that doesn't work out for you at first as a learning experience versus an unfortunate circumstance. Can you think of a situation where you fell victim to a memory drag? If you still have some skeletons in your closet that keep you stuck, clear them out! Isolate your bad memories and start reframing. Here is one more powerful tool that spiritual-preneurs carry in their self-leadership kit: hypnosis.

As mentioned above, hypnosis is often cited as one of the most effective ways to reprogram your subconscious mind. It clears out cellular memory and corrects any distorted neurological patterns that are compromising your performance. And a very practical benefit of this technique: you do not need to see an outside expert. In fact, all that is required for this gentle 'self-healing' is an audio recording from a reputable clinical hypnotherapist, your phone and some time, preferably in the evening as you are about to relax and fall asleep. For hypnosis to do its trick, you have to find a professional that 'clicks' with you, so to speak. Among other things, you have to find their voice soothing to listen to. I personally enjoy the recordings of Dr. Steve G. Jones, who built a successful practice in Hollywood, LA and worked with many celebrities over the years (Appendix A).

When it comes to energetic healing, spiritual-preneurs carry two additional tools in their spiritual self-leadership toolkit. These two tools are tapping, and an ancient Hawaiian forgiveness and a wealth prayer with a rather catchy name. Keep on reading to find out what that is. Both of these techniques gradually clear any residual energetic debris.

Clear Your Energy Through Tapping

Tap Your Way to Success was the title of a development workshop I attended in Dallas in 2013. It was a part of a larger leadership conference, but the value I drew from this event boils down to this technique: *Thought Field Therapy* (TFT). TFT also known as tapping was developed by a famous American psychologist Dr. Roger Callahan. There is an interesting story here to tell. Despite a successful, yet traditional clinical practice, Dr. Callahan suddenly realized there was something wrong with the bigger picture. He started to question the effectiveness of his current counselling methods and approaches, as his patients kept coming back to his counselling chair sometimes for decades. He asked himself this: "To what extent am I helping my patients, if they have been my clients for all these years"? This insight inspired him to look for alternative healing methods and ultimately led to the creation of the *Thought Field Therapy* or tapping.

This healing method produces fast results and is often compared to a psychological acupuncture. It involves tapping with the index and middle finger on certain energy points of the body called the Meridians (Appendix E). This system of energy points comes from a traditional Chinese medicine. Tapping on select meridians injects the body with new energy that is received and registered by your body as a healing code. Tapping has a healing effect because it rebalances the body's energetic system. Specifically, it releases blocked energy and eliminates internal perturbations that are caused by anything from suppressed negative feelings, past traumas, unresolved emotional issues and other emotional baggage. Scientists call these internal perturbations 'psychological reversal'.

Psychological reversal (PR) signals a reversed energy flow or a reversed polarity, to use a more scientific term. Tapping corrects this polarity reversal and eliminates any energy blockages by injecting fresh energy. What is interesting to note and lines up with our current discussion is that psychological reversal is an example of a self-sabotaging internal program that can be tapped out. This is what makes tapping another useful spiritual self-leadership tool.

Through a network of like-minded entrepreneurs, I became familiar with the work of Lynne McTaggart, an award-winning British journalist, author and a tapping practitioner. In her best-seller titled *Living the Field: Tapping into the Secret Force of the Universe*, Lynne provides a list of some of the more obvious signs of psychological reversal and their possible causes. These includes, but are not limited to, "negative self-talk, irritability, difficulty in accomplishing or doing, performance slump, self-sabotaging behavior, reversing concepts and numbers or being stuck in a particular area in life". Possible causes of psychological reversal are "system-overload and burnout, accumulation of toxins, negative intentions, medications, electromagnetic frequencies, traumas and others". Do any of these reversal signs and causes resonate with you? On a personal note, when I am over-worked, I start occasionally reversing the order of words in certain phrases. When a "tall broom" becomes a "brall toom", I know I am over-tired and need to take remedial action. To self-correct psychological reversals quickly, you can tap a few times with your index and middle finger under nose or on the side of your hand. This side of hand meridian is also known as the "karate chop" spot. Tap either of these two meridian points for a few seconds the moment you realize that you are dealing with a reversal situation and it will be cleared.

A key benefit of tapping is that it is easy to do and delivers fast results, including stress relief. Within minutes, it eliminates or at least diffuses most negative emotions such as anger or frustration. The healing principle behind tapping is the release of energy that is trapped within your energetic body. What caused this energy blockage? You may be surprised to learn that with every argument or a disagreement for instance, residual energy is created. If it is not cleared immediately, it gets stuck in your energetic body and disrupts its optimal functioning.

The release of this energetic residue or disturbance is so vital to our survival that nature has equipped some species with an automatic clearing system that kicks in right at the point of altercation. It is Eckhart Tolle who highlights and describes this fact in his best-seller *the Power of Now*, when he directs our attention to a behavioral pattern or a built-in response of certain animal species such as birds. Eckhart goes on to observe that when birds get into a physical altercation, they flap their wings several times before they fly off. They do this to get rid of any excess energy that accumulated as a result of the conflict. In other words, they shake off the energetic residue so that it does not get stuck and weigh them down. There is always something to learn from mother nature. Unfortunately, our coping mechanism does just the opposite. We humans have tendency to sweep anything unpleasant under the carpet to avoid the pain of dealing with it. Most of us avoid confrontation and procrastinate on dealing with important issues.

I invite you to ask yourself honestly: what do you think is the state of your energetic body? If you are running away from resolving something, which you know needs to be resolved; if you are an argumentative type who likes to start verbal fights, you are doing yourself a disservice. You are creating unnecessary energetic havoc that leads to blockages and underachievement. As you create through energy, any energetic blockages will translate into your diminished creative power.

What do spiritual-preneurs do in instances like this? They integrate tapping into their daily routine to prevent any energy blockages and to tap out any lingering energetic clutter. They know that a simple tapping exercise has the power to release any suppressed energy in your body and facilitate forward movement. Let's now take a closer look at a basic tapping sequence to give you a concrete example. Please note that Dr. Callahan's *Thought Field Therapy* as a clinical approach goes well beyond this simple tapping exercise. Treatment of each individual trauma or phobia for instance involves the application of a unique tapping sequence that was designed to treat that one particular issue. While the basic tapping sequence introduced below can be 'self-administered', any more advanced healing applications of TFT require a trained clinical practitioner to be effective. If tapping is something that is of interest, I invite you to do a more thorough research on the topic and consult with a clinically trained practitioner.

***

The Tapping Etiquette

As with all practical approaches, the only way to grasp this technique is through experimentation. I encourage you to find some tapping videos on YouTube as you read through the instructions given in the section below. Brad Yates has become quite known in this sphere and has made tapping more accessible as a self-treatment (see Appendix A). His YouTube segments are about 7 minutes long and are designed to address different issues or emotional states, from fear, to guilt, anger, procrastination etc. As is the case with any method, tapping is more effective if you set an intention. You also have to be patient with the process, as you may need to go through a few rounds of tapping before you get the hang of it and start witnessing tangible results.

You may alternatively find that this technique does not suit you at all, and that is ok too. We are all different and that is a beautiful thing!

BASIC CLEARING SEQUENCE

The basic clearing sequence involves tapping a set of Meridian points shown in Appendix E. To fully benefit from this section, consult this Appendix and get familiar with the relevant energy points for this clearing exercise. In addition to the meridians in the diagram, this routine also involves tapping four additional energy points on your hands (described further below). For some of you, it may be easier to pull up an image from Google as we speak. Just enter 'tapping and meridians' into the search window and look for results under images.

In the basic tapping sequence, you first tap on all relevant meridian points with your right hand, you then perform a 9-GAMUT procedure, and finally tap the same points with your left hand. Breathe in and breathe out, and you have completed the basic sequence. Unless otherwise specified, tap each point about 5-7 times, using your index and middle fingers. Start tapping these points with your right hand in this specific order: top of head, beginning of eyebrow, side of eye, under eye, under nose, center of chin, collarbone, under arm, karate chop spot, thumb, index finger, ring (4th) finger and little finger (always tapping the outside of each finger). The 9-gamut sequence is described below separately as it is an effective relaxation technique as a stand-alone piece. Perform this clearing sequence daily for at least week or longer to see if tapping has any positive effect on you and your overall well-being.

TAPPING in a BUSINESS CONTEXT

The interesting thing is, tapping as a technique has a broad application and this includes the business context. To this point, the standard 9-GAMUT process, also known as the "9-gamut floor-to-ceiling eye-roll", is a powerful relaxation technique that can be performed quickly before an important business meeting, presentation, or an interview. The 9-GAMUT process involves tapping a specific meridian point called the gamut spot, which is accompanied by a specific 9-step floor-to-ceiling eye-roll movement. If this process sounds a bit strange at first, please remember its clinical psychology background. Now, let's carry on.

The gamut spot is located on the back of your hand between the knuckles of your pinky finger and your ring finger (4th finger), about an inch down towards your wrist. Here is how you do the 9-gamut exercise. You tap the gamut spot with your right hand first while going through the 9-step process below. For the tapping to be effective, you have to perform all 9 actions listed. When done, you tap the same meridian with your left hand and repeat.

9-gamut floor to ceiling eye-roll

1. Eyes open
2. Eyes closed
3. Eyes down left
4. Eyes down right
5. Roll eyes in a complete circle
6. Roll eyes in a complete circle the other way
8. Hum a few seconds of a tune aloud
9. Count aloud from one to five
10. Hum aloud again
11. Repeat on the other hand

To give you a sense of how powerful tapping is, here is list of some issues resulting from energy blockages, and what happens when these blockages are released through tapping.

THUMB = SELF-WORTH: energy imbalance through negative thinking

When blocked, it causes lethargy, grief and low energy.
When tapped, it increases vitality and positivity.

INDEX Finger = LETTING GO: energy imbalance through hanging on to grief and guilt
When blocked, it causes nostalgia.
When tapped, it releases emotions that hold us living in the past.

MIDDLE Finger = BONDING: energy imbalance through being unhappy with self and others
When blocked, it produces feelings of self-esteem.
When tapped, it releases feelings of inferiority and increases personal power.

LITTLE Finger = UNCONDITIONAL LOVE: energy imbalance through lack of love for self and others
When blocked, it results in selfishness and loneliness.
When tapped, it removes limited thinking, opens up consciousness and improves long-term memory.

KARATE Chop Point = TRUST
When blocked, it results in lack of confidence and feelings of self-hate.

When tapped, it removes self-doubt, feelings of low self-esteem and improves self-confidence.

GAMUT point = CONNECTION
When blocked, there is an inability to express emotions, including love.
When tapped, it improves self-esteem and opens up to emotional interactions with others.

Are you starting to see the value of this energetic technique? The above information has been adapted from Silvia Hartmann's book titled *Adventures in EFT*. EFT or *Emotional Freedom Technique* is a tapping variation that I will introduce you to in a minute. But first…

Time for another testimonial. While the whole concept of tapping, including the 9-gamut process, sounded odd to me at first, but I kept an open-mind. After all, Dr. Callahan's technique received endless praises over the years and many of his patients were finally freed of phobias that may have seemed incurable to them at first. To my surprise, after only a few tapping sessions of the basic clearing sequence, I felt lighter, more energized and my overall energy field intensified. I felt more present, more grounded in my power and it was not just me that felt renewed. Others started to notice and comment! Whatever the tapping method corrected internally, I felt better, stronger and certain things started to unfold for me with more ease. If you wish to carry on this conversation for a bit longer, you can refer to Appendix D for more tapping tips.

***

The Emotional Freedom Technique

As pointed out earlier, the *Emotional Freedom Technique* (EFT) is a tapping variation that combines tapping with positive affirmations. EFT is also a form of psychological acupuncture that can optimize your emotional health by neutralizing negative emotions and removing past emotional pain. In this technique, you tap with the same two fingers (index and ring) to input kinetic energy into specific meridians. You can target EFT sessions at specific issues from past traumatic events, addictions, fears etc.

Below are some basic tapping affirmations that you can say aloud while tapping the top of head and collarbone meridians. Many more affirmations are provided in Appendix B. When tapping is combined with positive statements said aloud, a cerebral resonance is created in your subconscious, which intensifies the healing effect of the exercise. Consequently, this resonance clears any emotional blocks from your body's bioenergetic system.

"I fully love and accept myself"!

"It's like me to be a winner! It's like me to be abundant"!

"That's the NEW me and that's the way I am NOW! Abundant and happy!"

If there is one key take-way from our tapping, it is this quick and effective exercise below. In an instant, it will release trapped negativity and you make you feel lighter!

INSTRUCTIONS: Anchor your new vision of self on an image or visualize your goal. Keep tapping your collarbone meridian for a few minutes, while you repeat the phrase below aloud several times in a row. Although it may sound simple, tapping has a profound transformative and healing effect. You would be surprised how many people suffer from a lack of self-love, for instance. Here is what you do next. Tap with your right hand on the left collarbone spot, then tap the right collarbone spot with your left hand, as you say the affirmation below. Do not stress about getting it perfect.

Rather focus on your goal and get into the feeling behind affirmation, injecting some new energy into your system. You cannot do this process incorrectly; in fact, the only thing that will ruin the result is doubt and worry.

I FULLY LOVE AND ACCEPT MYSELF!

***

Forgive the Hawaiian Way

Last but not least, a clearing technique that that comes to you from the very green and blue beautiful Hawaii. Aloha! Allow me to introduce you to Ho'oponopono, a Hawaiian cleansing and forgiveness method and a wealth prayer, abbreviated to HOP for the remainder of our discussion. Everything in life has a story and the story behind HOP is quite illuminating indeed. The story tells of a clinical therapist born in Hawaii, Dr. Haleakala Hew Len, who supposedly cured an entire ward of mentally-ill patients with minimal doctor-patient interaction, while working mainly with the Ho'oponopono technique. HOP's effectiveness rests in the fact that, like hypnosis and bio-sync, it clears (heals) at the level of cellular memory and thus reprograms. What is unique about this technique is that it also clears memories and issues that span across lineages and generations. This is what Dr. Hew Len calls ancestral memories. The subject of ancestral memories is well beyond the scope of this book. Know, however, that according Dr. Hew Len and many other experts, unresolved memories are your direct enemy. Ancestral memories are even worse, as they result from generations of accumulated negativity that can hold an entire generation (nation) in an undesirable pattern. Your memories are an integral part of your internal hard-drive and need to be cleared if you think that you are experiencing a case of an internal resistance. Dr. Hew Len further explains that once you clear all individual and collective negative memories, you are able to connect with the Divinity and are ready to hear the Divine inspiration that comes from within. This statement reflects my personal experience, thank you Hawaii!

Another unique feature of this Hawaiian technique is that it is also a forgiveness process. And at this point of our discussion, I do not have to highlight the benefits of forgiveness or its corresponding frequency. From this perspective, "Thank you!" and "I forgive you!" are two most vibrationally powerful sentences. Once you grant forgiveness where it needs to be granted, including forgiveness of self, you are freed, cleared and closer to the state of 'allowing'. There is no more internal resistance or hindrance when it comes to your progress. In this sense, this clearing work is your fast-past to your manifestations!

Spiritual-preneurs made the Hawaiian prayer and other energetic clearing techniques a regular part of their self-leadership ritual. They know, based on their direct experience, that this clearing process puts them in a state of greater clarity and allows them to perceive, receive and interpret the creative inspiration that shines in! To reiterate Dr. Hew Len's claims, the only way to hear the Divine or the life force within you is when you get clear or when you are "zero". At zero, you have an expanded clarity and an unobstructed line of communication with your spiritual Self or your divinity. The opportunity for transformation with this technique comes from the realization that you co-created your current reality and are responsible for fixing it. Your self-forgiveness also carries a healing element.

As an extension of this reasoning, when Dr. Hew Len was treating these mentally-ill patients, he first assumed full responsibility for manifesting this situation in his life. He integrated the forgiveness method into his approach and over the span of about 2 years, most of these patients were gradually released. The Ho'oponopono prayer is a forgiveness and clearing process. For an increased benefit, repeat this four-sentence prayer out-loud 4 times, while focusing on a specific issue.

I AM SORRY. I LOVE YOU. PLEASE FORGIVE ME. THANK YOU.

Here is the underlying message behind these words that you are communicating to the Divine, spiritual realm or the universal intelligence: "I am sorry for not understanding everything and for not being aware. I am are sorry for unwillingly co-creating the situation that I am facing. I acknowledge all of my decisions and actions and take a hundred percent responsibility for co-creating every aspect of my current life circumstance. I am asking for forgiveness for my limited vision and for getting disconnected from the source. I am forgiving others and myself. I proclaim love to that which created me as well as gratitude to the universe and the life force that permeates through it and through my entire body". There is no need to say these words aloud, but these are the thoughts that are in the backdrop of your mind as you recite the prayer. Feel free to reword the above script to meet your personal preferences and align with your personal beliefs.

Like some of the other energetic clearing tools that we introduced thus far, the Ho'oponopono method is another effective way to clear any counter-intentions, limiting beliefs and negative past memories. On a personal note, integrating this forgiveness prayer into my spiritual practice brought me more clarity on how best to utilize my unique talents for the benefit of others and beyond the scope of my primary business. It also helped me achieve greater internal alignment and facilitated a more effective communication with my spiritual Self. I revert to this prayer daily and at times, I use its extended version that was introduced by Morrnah Simeona, another energetic healer from Hawaii.

MORRNAH'S FORGIVENESS PRAYER

In 1980, Morrnah Simeona, a national treasure of Hawaii, introduced the Ho'oponopono method at a local convention center and then travelled the world teaching this forgiveness technique to others. Since this prayer is publicly available, I am including it here for your benefit. It is another tool of the spiritual-MBA toolkit. Unlike its shorter version above, Dr. Joe Vitale recommends using Morrnah's extended prayer for more stubborn or lingering issues and outdated beliefs.

**

"SPIRIT, SUPERCONSCIOUS!"

Please locate the origin of my feelings and thoughts of ... *insert whatever issue, past memory or limiting belief you are clearing, e.g. scarcity mindse*t.

Please take every level, layer, area and aspect of my being to this origin. Analyze it and resolve it perfectly according to God's truth.

Come through all generations of time and eternity, healing every incident and its appendages based on the origin. Please do it according to God's will, until I am at the present, filled with light and truth.

God's peace and love, forgiveness of myself for my incorrect perceptions. Forgiveness of every person, place, circumstances and events, which contributed to this: these feelings and thoughts".

I love you. I am sorry. Please forgive me. Thank you!

Morrnah recommends repeating this prayer aloud 4 times, focusing either on the same or a different issue every time. At the end of each round, take a deep breath in and out and say the shorter 4-phrase prayer - **I love you, I am sorry, please forgive me, thank you** - before continuing on to the next round. Your sequence then is Morrnah's prayer, the 4-phrase prayer, breath in, breath out and repeat! As is with any positive affirmations or prayers, by articulating them out loud, you are registering your words more deeply within your subconscious, and thus enhance their creative and transformative effect.

As pointed out earlier, the Ho'oponopono process is believed to connect you to your own light or divinity because it clears all negative individual and ancestral memories. Moreover, as you forgive the various parts of your Self, your limiting beliefs and destructive patterns, eventually dissolve dissipate. When this happens, your inner and outer worlds regain more balance and harmony. This circles back to our central idea that wealth is created from within and that is where you need to start! If you heal and build yourself internally first, you will regain and fortify your power to create in the external world anything that your mind has imagined and conceived of. Like with any process, faith is another critical component. You have to do keep doing your part and keeping clear, while trusting that the Divinity within you will do its own in resolving the unresolved and setting you on a clear path!

As mentioned throughout, spiritual-preneurs are committed to a process of continuous learning & self-development. This process includes regular clearing work so that they stay energetically "at zero", clear of the negative and able to perceive any intuitive messages. This is not always an easy task to accomplish. And the C+3P formula discussed earlier applies here too. You need to remain patient and persevere in order to witness any tangible results. It can take several weeks or even months to get through all the clearing work that you may require at the moment. In some cases, the involvement of a professional is highly recommended. My goal was to simply broaden your repertoire of spiritually-inspired tools. Decide for yourself which of the technique presented suits you best and start experimenting. This brings me to the end of our conversation on energetic healing. While I could easily continue our conversation, the point was to give you a few quick references and some foundational knowledge that we can build on in subsequent volumes.

Very shortly, I will introduce you to one more system that provides a unique perspective and sheds some insightful light on opportunities and challenges related to a particular life-path. But first, let's review the broader context within which we operate, including some additional universal principles that are critical to any level of success and happiness.

***

From Corporate to Spiritual Law

The world in which we all live is governed by a myriad of natural laws. These laws are as impartial as the *Law of Gravity*. We have already looked at several of these laws, including the *Law of Detachment* and the *Law of Attraction*. There are many other higher laws at work that you need to be aware of and live in harmony with, especially if you wish to manifest all the love, prosperity and happiness that you seek. There are too many of these laws to name them all in this book, but the most pertinent once have been included in our conversation. For a more complete picture, you can study the books of Dan Millman and Deepak Chopra and other references suggested in Appendix A.

If you take time to understand these natural principles and align your code of conduct accordingly, you will be much better equipped to create all the success and abundance that you can imagine. Everything is possible in life, as long as you have the right attitude and the right set of tools. Archimedes, the Greek mathematician, physicist, inventor and astronomer comments:

"If you give someone strong enough levers, they can move the Earth".

In this regard, these spiritual or natural laws are your success-levers and your guide-posts on your way to the top. Here is a partial list of the first 11 that are particularly relevant to success and achievement.

The Law of Karma

The Law of Choices

The Law of Giving and Receiving

The Law of Desire and Intention

The Law of Discipline

The Law of Detachment

The Law of Action & Compensation

The Law of Least Effort

The Law of Intuition

The Law of Higher Will

The Law of Responsibility

I invite you to get intimately familiar with this topic and Deepak Chopra's *Seven Spiritual Laws of Success* is an excellent starting point. My objective was to raise your awareness of the broader universal context and its own set of guidelines that we need to align with to experience boundless happiness, health and abundance.

The LAWS of SUCCESS

If I asked you to name one person that influenced you the most and helped you grow, who would that be? It does not have to be someone that you physically spent time with, but someone whose work or philosophy made an impact on you, someone who made you think or act differently. Do you know who would that person be? For me, one of those mentor-figures is Napoleon Hill and his famous book called *The Law of Success in 16 Lessons*. I have made several references to this classic that is a staple in my home library.

As mentioned earlier, Napoleon Hill was hired by one of the most successful Scottish-American industrialists, a business magnet and a philanthropist of the Gilded Age (early 1900s). Mr. Carnegie proposed to Napoleon an important but peculiar assignment: he asked him to study self-made millionaires and based on his findings, create a philosophy of success. To carry out his mandate, Napoleon interviewed people that rose to the ranks of millionaires by their own efforts, and then distilled his findings into a 600-page-long philosophy of success. This philosophy is comprised of 16 distinct laws of success. If you wish to build a happy and prosperous life, study and live these principles with every breath. Why? Listen to what I have to say next!

***

The Spiritual and Success Law Convergence

It is not a coincidence that Napoleon's laws of success converge with the higher spiritual principles. In fact, while the spiritual laws act as broader guidelines, Napoleon's success principles are their corresponding behavioral or attitudinal representations. Let's look at some examples so that you see this point more clearly. The universal laws are italicized while Napoleon's success principles are in bold.

The *Law of Non-Judgement* demands what Napoleon Hill calls an **Accurate Thought**. Accurate thought requires that you carefully separate facts from opinions and thoroughly analyze all aspects of a situation or a subject at hand, and only then form an opinion.

As the *Law of Choices* suggests, we create in every moment. It is up to us to divert our energies to the right cause and ensure that we are creating only in the positive. This requires the formulation of what Napoleon Hill calls a **Definite Chief Aim** (singleness of purpose or your main goal). You also need to tap into your **Imagination** so that you can first envision your goal and construct it in your mind. You then need a harmonious **Cooperation** (Mastermind) with other people and that calls for the development of a **Pleasing Personality**.

The *Law of Action* requires **Initiative** and **Leadership**, **Enthusiasm** and **Imagination**. It also calls for discipline and **Self-Control**.

The *Law of Responsibility* mandates the **Habit of Saving** and the **Habit of Doing More than Paid For**.

The above examples, which we could easily expand on, underscore one important truth. There is a core set of principles, behaviors and attitudes that you need to emulate, if you wish to build and live a life of love, health, success, happiness and abundance. While different authors or gurus may name these principles differently, on the behavioral level, they all refer to a certain 'code of conduct' that these laws imply, and by which all spiritual-preneurs live. I invite you to do the same if success and wealth is what you are in the pursuit of! For the sake of completeness, here are Napoleon's 16 laws of success named in no particular order of importance.

1. A Definite Chief Aim
2. Self- Confidence
3. The Habit of Saving
4. Initiative and Leadership
5. Imagination
6. Enthusiasm
7. Self-Control
8. Habit of Doing More than Paid For
9. Pleasing Personality
10. Accurate Thought
11. Concentration
12. Co-operation
13. Failure
14. Tolerance
15. The Golden Rule
16. Mastermind

What Are You Here to Do?

We are getting almost to the last segment of our journey together. So far, I have introduced you to a variety of useful tools and approaches that will help you build a strong foundation for lasting wealth, happiness and abundance. Many of the strategies discussed are your 'success levers' and are therefore an essential part of the spiritual-MBA toolkit. But, like with any other recipe, you have to use all of the suggested ingredients to cook up the perfect meal! Cut corners and take shortcuts and your beef bourguignon will not be the same as Julia Child's. The same applies to any self-leadership toolkit. It is only powerful to the extent that it is used!

At this point, I want to re-direct your attention to the topic of life purpose, which is the most important journey you will ever take. As the *Law of Dharma* (purpose) dictates, "we have taken manifestation in the physical form to fulfill a purpose" (Chopra). This statement is based on the premise disclosed at the beginning of this book. A premise that we are spiritual beings first and our human physical incarnation comes second. Part of our physical experience is our deep-seated desire to discover and live out our life-purpose, as that is our only path to fulfillment! As Deepak Chopra further comments:

"Everyone has a purpose in life, a unique gift or a special talent to give to others. And when we blend this unique talent with service to others, we experience the ECTASY and EXULTATION of our own Spirit, which is the ultimate goal of all goals".

**

You probably figured by now that the expression of your special inner gifts or your life purpose does not always unfold easy. It may take little time for some and even a few decades for others to discover their life's mission, passion and purpose. As one would expect, your spiritual journey entails a set of challenges that test you along the way and ultimately make you grow and become stronger. According to Dan Millman, a personal development expert, lecturer and author, the degree to which we fulfill our potential and live out our life purpose depends on how we respond to challenges that we meet on our path. This is essentially Tony Robbins's key proposition of re-framing. As we will see shortly, each life-path has its unique set of challenges and opportunities.

Without a doubt, understanding the context within which you operate along with an increased awareness of the specific lessons inherent to your life-path will make you more effective and greatly augment your chances of winning at this game of life! As Dan Millman concludes:

> **"We are given the playing field, but we choose how to play the game".**

The next few pages briefly speak to this very point and introduce the life-path system proposed by Dan Millman.

***

The Life-Path System

Now let's turn your attention to one last formula that will show you how and where to focus your life's energies and efforts and what pitfalls to avoid. I am talking about the life-purpose system, which is numerology-based system that calculates a specific life-path number based on one's date of birth. This 'personal life-path code' and the information that comes with it provides a personal context for the application of the spiritual-preneurship toolkit introduced in this book.

It comes down to this: over the course of our lives, we all face a specific set of challenges that are inherent to our unique life-path. Our life journey mirrors the lessons that we need to go through to grow and reach our potential. Some spiritual gurus take this claim one step further and believe that every challenge and circumstance that we encounter has been pre-selected by our Spirit before manifesting in this physical form. Nevertheless, the value of the life-path system is undeniable. As its architect Dan Millman points out:

"While self-analysis can generate the impulse to change, the life-purpose system provides the means" to bring about transformation".

**

Due to its accuracy and effectiveness, I have integrated the life-path system into my life coaching work. This approach in particular provided some invaluable insights with respect to my own life journey. Specifically, it revealed what areas of my life needed 'extra care' and what areas where my strongest success levers "on the way to the summit of my own mountain" (Millman). Working with the life-purpose system and the higher spiritual laws increased my understanding of certain behavioral patterns in myself that were not serving my higher purpose and that I was blind to before. Dan Millman's guidance provided another set of data that connected the dots and led to several transformative insights. When I applied these insights to specific challenges, transformative outcomes followed. I admit, the accurateness and insightfulness of the information shared in the life-path system shocked me, as did the stroke of serendipity with which even this book showed up in my life.

It is helpful to view the life-path approach as a giant microscope that strategically magnifies and exposes some of your most hidden strategic levers or unidentified liabilities. In line with our discussion, it also directs your attention to potential cobwebs that may have accumulated over time and need to be cleared out. Only then will you be ready to build a strong foundation for boundless wealth, happiness and achieve a lifetime of fulfillment. If leveraged properly, the life-path system has the potential to accelerate your personal and professional growth and also that of your bank account!

MEANING BEHIND NUMBERS

If you paid attention in your math class, you may remember learning about Pythagoras, a Greek philosopher who believed and taught that number was the essence of all things. Pythagoras mystically associated numbers with virtues, colors and many other ideas (Millman). As indicated earlier, the life-path system is a number-based formula that has the potential to bring your life into a crystal-clear focus. Your individual lessons and learnings are based on a personal code derived from one's date of birth. For example, if you are born on September 12, 1978, your life path number is 37/10. To get your life-path number, add up all the digits in your birthday.

1+2+0+9+1+9+7+8 = 37

The second step entails adding the two single digits of your first total, which is 3+7=10. Your life-path number is their combination or 37/10 and can be further reduced to a primary life-path number 1.

If your birthday falls on November 10, 1978, the numbers you are adding are 1+0+1+0+1+9+7+8 = 27. 2=7=9 so your life-path combination is 27/9. This can be further reduced to a primary life-path number 9.

For those born on February 12, 2018:
1+2+0+2+2+0+1+8=16. You are working energies of a

16/7 combination and your primary life-path number is 7.

From Liabilities to Strengths: From Chaos to Clarity

As you can observe from the list below, each primary life-path number aligns with certain key dimensions and focuses the energies of that number on a specific set of issues. As Dan Millman explains:

"The numbers do reflect inborn promise, because with each number come deeply rooted psychological drivers toward the fulfillment of our destiny. Along with the inner drives associated with our number come subconscious fears of success, fears of abusing that which we are here to express. The dynamic tension between our drives and our fears creates the theatre of our life".

What does this all mean for you? First, take a moment to calculate your primary life-path number and refer to the list below to see what potential challenge areas you may need to master first in order to self-actualize and live out your life purpose.

Let me provide a few examples for the sake of clarity. Those working the primary life-path number 9 have to work through issues of integrity and wisdom in the world. But first, they have to find these higher principles within them. Number 7s have to work through issues of trust and openness. They have to learn how to overcome issues of paranoia and isolation, start trusting their inner most feelings and eventually open up to others.

Below is a high-level description of key energies and areas of focus associated with each of the primary life-path numbers (0-9). This information was adapted from Dan Millman's fabulously insightful book titled *the Life You Were Born to Live*. If you are still unsure of what your true inner gifts and talents are, or where to focus your efforts, Dan's work can lead you to some transformative revelations and insights.

Primary Number 1: Creativity & Confidence
Primary Number 2: Cooperation & Balance
Primary Number 3: Expression & Sensitivity
Primary Number 4: Stability & Process
Primary Number 5: Freedom & Discipline
Primary Number 6: Vision & Acceptance
Primary Number 7: Trust & Openness

Primary Number 8: Abundance & Power
Primary Number 9: Integrity & Wisdom
Primary Number 0: Inner Gifts

The key take-away is this: the energies of each number can be worked either in the positive or the negative. In the negative, their misguided use can lead to a deviation from one life's purpose, stagnation and even possible self-sabotage. Taking the right preventative steps starts with raising your level of awareness of your primary number and the challenges inherent to that life path. You also need to raise your awareness of any hidden talents and potential growth areas that are unique to your life path and that you may not have yet explored.

Let's look at another example to further illustrate the nature of insights gained from working with Dan Millman's framework. We ca continue with the 27/9 life-path combination further reduced to 9. As Dan points out, people working the primary life-path number 9 "exude depth, charisma and wisdom based on their heartfelt trust in the Spirit working through them". If number 'nines' work the energies of their number in the positive, they make the best leaders who live in alignment with the higher principles. However, if these folks work the energies in the negative, they risk losing sight of their higher purpose and can feel "cut off, lonely, locked in the mind and out of touch with their heart and intuitive guidance". In the negative, the 9s become "the best fanatics, preachers or eternal seekers" (Millman). Do you see the range of possible life outcomes? We can go literally from good to bad, depending on how we leverage our respective life-path energies. Luckily, we hold the master key and get to make a new choice every moment. Since the life-path information is proprietary, I strongly encourage you to get a copy of Dan's book if the nature of insights seems of value based on what was provided. At the very least, it can serve as an effective guide book for your *Incredible Life* movie! Let's look at a few more energy highlights before we conclude.

People working the primary life-path number 1 have a tremendous creative potential, but in order to discover and then nurture this talent, they have to first overcome issues of insecurity and possible addictions. When they work their life-path number in the positive, they "channel high energy and inspiration into creativity and service and feel secure with self". But, when they work their life-path energy in the negative, "they feel blocked, stuck, they feel inferior, lethargic, insecure and possibly addicted". If you are a 37/10, you are here to work through issues of creativity, while learning to trust your wise and beautiful Spirit in yourself and others.

Primary 8: In the positive, "8s make the best philanthropists. In the negative, they make the best passive-aggressives".

Primary 6: In the positive, "6s make the best judges. In the negative, they make the best perfectionists".

In addition to raising your level of awareness, the life-path system provides a series of concrete strategies that can turn your liabilities into strengths. These come in the form of specific action steps associated with each life path and entail some inner alignment work as well as harmonization with the natural laws previously discussed. The life-path system is an extremely effective framework to use, as it allows you to better focus your personal development efforts and tap into your untapped potential. And as Deepak Chopra further attests:

"The Life-Purpose System as expressed in Dan Millman's new book is absolutely amazing in its PREDICTIVE value. It will help you sort out the conflicts in your life and guide you on the path to fulfillment".

Conclusion

"Whether you believe that you can or cannot, either way you are right"!

~Napoleon Hill~

**

Whether you believe that you can or cannot leverage the information shared in this book to enhance your current level of success and happiness, either way, you are right! What you do with this information and a new set of tools is completely up to you. As was mentioned earlier, even the most valuable piece of information or a nugget of wisdom is only useful to the extent that it is used, applied and leveraged. It is up to you to 'digest' the information and tools that were introduced. It is up to you to apply them, to test them out or to shelve the book and never look at it again. Just remember that you create in each moment, so make sure that you are making the right choice!

The *Spiritual-MBA* self-development series is an exciting new beginning that holds a tremendous potential. It is a new collective journey that will hopefully touch lives of many, that will accomplish many positive things and create a hypnotizing spiritual ripple effect!

The Spiritual MBA is . . .

An insightful, PRACTICAL SPIRITUALITY pocketbook that reveals an entire suite of spiritually-inspired self-leadership tools and tactics.

It is the first of its kind LIFE-SUCCESS companion created by a passionate enlightened entrepreneur that gives you an opportunity to pause, reflect, re-imagine your life and create a new, more refreshing and fulfilling VISION for yourself. It gives you a ROADMAP and some tools to re-invent yourself based on your innermost desires, talents and your life's purpose.

It is a PLATFORM to promote the unique voice, experiences and successes of other enlightened entrepreneurs, business leaders and spiritual-preneurs! It is also a spiritually-inspired self-leadership framework that can help you build a robust foundation for LASTING wealth and happiness.

It is a MOVEMENT that connects, inspires and builds across the globe. A social and virtual global movement to ROLE-MODEL, empower and create a positive global IMPACT. This starts with living by the higher principles and those of spiritual-preneurship described herein. This also means actively managing your SPIRITUAL FOOTPRINT on a daily basis and acting in alignment with the Golden Rule.

To conclude our discussion, I trust that you found this book a worth-while investment and a useful resource that will allow you to play the best possible role in your own theatre of life! I equally hope that I have given you some useful tools and ideas to further enhance your *Incredible Life* movie script and produce a real work of art or an Oscar nominee!! You certainly deserve it!

My objective was to create an easy-to-read book that is informative, insightful, practical and as entertaining as a self-help book can be! The information, tools and techniques introduced to you herein have the potential to lead you to transformational breakthroughs in your life, both personal and professional. Digest this information, integrate it, apply it consistently. And when you do:

"Witness the MIRACULOUS"!

~Deepak Chopra~

**

I encourage you to keep this book handy and experiment with this material freely and frequently. Keep detailed records of your journey, insights and the results you witness. If you have any questions, you know where to find me. Until the next volume! I leave you with two more inspiring quotes, with the first by Napoleon Hill.

"Far too many people spend their entire lives waiting for that GLORIOUS day when the PERFECT opportunity presents itself to them. Too late, they realize that each day held opportunity for those who sought it out! [...] Do not waste another minute"!

**

And finally, a powerful concluding statement by a contemporary guru on the subject of peak performance and human potential, Mr. Tony Robbins.

"Now I am the voice! I will LEAD, not follow! I will believe, not doubt! I will CREATE, not destroy! I am a leader! Defy the odds! Set a standard! STEP UP"!

In Wealth and Happiness,
The Spiritual MBA

Acknowledgments

I would like to extend a very special thank you to my amazing parents Bozena and Marian, without whom I would not be who I am today! Thank you for your love, support and for believing in me even when my plans didn't always make sense to you! I love you! A big kiss to my brother Marian and his lovely family!

A special thank you goes to my graphic Designer Yoshi.

A million thanks to my dear friends who have provided constructive feedback during this writing and creation process. Many thanks to Kevin Malone, Rhonda Yagod, Cliff Hecht, Rick Tessier and Danya Backman!

Thank you to my dear friend Debbie Lawless-Miller who made me see my own light!

And lastly, my eternal gratitude to the Spirit that guided me on this incredible journey!

***

About the Author

Vladimira Juskova is a successful entrepreneur, life coach, writer and a spiritual-preneur! Over the past few years, Vladimira has been building a global advisory firm with activities in the commodities sector. Aside from creating and managing new businesses and enticing joint venture projects with her partner and their team, Vladimira's passion is to inspire and guide others on their own journey to success.

She gained invaluable insights into the areas of organizational and human capital development during her almost decade-long career in Executive Leadership Development at the Rotman School of Management, University of Toronto, a premier Canadian research university.

Vladimira holds a graduate degree in Adult Education (M.Ed.) in Curriculum Design (Brock University, Canada) and a graduate degree in Business Administration (MBA) from the University of Toronto. She is a certified Human Resources professional and a certified energetic healer. In her *Spiritual MBA* handbook, Vladimira draws on her own experiences as a female entrepreneur and introduces an entire toolbox of spiritually-inspired success strategies focused on building external value from within. Vladimira was recognized by the *International Society for Performance Improvement* for her contributions to leadership development. She was a content contributor in a book on integrated curriculum and a research assistant on a book project in comparative children's literature (*Recycling Red Riding Hood,* Professor Sandra L. Beckett).

**

OTHER PUBLICATIONS & AWARDS

Creating Standards-Based & Integrated Curriculum. Professor Susan Drake (chapter contribution)

Leading the Way: Leadership Development Program recognized by the *International Society for Performance Improvement* in 2010 (program design, management & evaluation).

***

Appendix A: Bibliography

CITED BOOKS

Ariely, Daniel. *Predictably Irrational*. New York, Harper Collins, 2008.

Allen, James. *As a Man Thinketh & From Poverty to Power*. New York, Jeremy P. Tarcher/Penguin, 2008.

Bristol, Claude. *The Magic of Believing*. New York, Pocket Books, 1969.

Brown, Henry Harrison. *Dollars Want Me. The New Road to Opulence*. San Francisco, 1903.

Byrne, Rhonda. *The Secret*. New York, Atria Books, 2006.

Callahan, Roger. *Tapping the Healer Within*. Ebook.

Chopra, Deepak. *The Seven Spiritual Laws of Success*. San Rafael, CA, Amber-Allen Publishing, 1994.

Clear, James. *The Habits Guide: How to Build Good Habits and Break the Bad Ones*. Digital.

Collier, Robert. *The Secret of the Ages*. E-Book.

Gikandi, David Cameron. *Happy Pocket Full of Money*. Xlibris Corporation, 2008.

Denton, Elizabeth A., & Mitroff, Ian. *A Spiritual Audit of Corporate America*. Jossey-Bass, 1999.

Gladwell, Malcolm. *Outliers. The Story of Success*. New York, Little, Brown & Company, 2008.

Gladwell, Malcolm. Blink. *The Power of Thinking Without Thinking*. New York, Little, Brown and Company, 2005.

Hicks, Esther & Jerry, *Ask and It Is Given. Learning to Manifest Your Desires*. New York, Hay House Inc., 2004.

Hill, Napoleon. *Think and Grow Rich*. New York, Jeremy P. Tarcher/Penguin, 2005.

Hill, Napoleon. *The Law of Success in 16 Lessons*. New York, Jeremy P. Tarcher/Penguin, 2008.

Hill, Napoleon. *The Master-Key to Riches*. New York, Ballantine Books, 1982.

Klinger, Sharon Anne, & Taylor, Sandra Anne. *The Akashic Tarot*. Hay House Inc, 2017.

Kotter, John P. *What Leaders Really Do*. Boston, Harvard Business Review Press, 1999.

Latham, Gary. *Becoming the Evidence-based Manager. Making the Science of Management Work for You*. Boston & London, Davies-Black, 2009.

Millman, Dan. *The Life You Were Born to Live*. Tiburon, CA, H J Kramer & New World Library, 1993.

Schwartz, David J. *The Magic of Thinking Big*. New York, A Fireside Book, 2007.

Maltz, Maxwell, MD. *The New Psycho-Cybernetics*. New York, Prentice Hall Press, 2001.

McTaggart, Lynne. *Living the Field. Tapping into the Secret Code of the Universe*. Audiobook.

Roger, Jim & Patton, Bruce and Ury, William. *Getting to Yes. How to Negotiate Agreements without Giving in.* London, Penguin, 2011.

Tolle, Eckhart. *The Power of Now.* London, Penguin, 1997.

Tolle, Eckhart. *A New Earth.* London, Penguin, 2005.

Vitale, Joe. *Awakened Millionaire. The Manifesto for Spiritual Wealth.* E-book.

Vitale, Joe. *The Greatest Money-Making Secret in History.* E-book.

Vitale Joe & Dr. Ihaleakala Hew Len. *Zero Limits. The Secret Hawaiian System for Wealth, Health, Peace & More.* Kindle Edition.

Virtue, Doreen. *Angel Therapy.* Cards.

Virtue, Doreen. *Angel Numbers 101.* Kindle Edition.

Ziglar, Zig. *See you at the Top.* Gretna, Pelican Publishing Company, 2017.

Ziglar, Zig. *Born to Win.* Made for Success Publishing, 2014. Kindle Edition

Wattles, Wallace. *The Science of Getting Rich.* Audiobook.

***

RECOMMENDED BOOKS

Barnum, PT. *The Art of Getting or Golden Rules for Making Money.*

Canfield, Jack. *The Success Principles.*

Dr. Dyer, Dwayne, W. *Wish Fulfilled. Mastering the Art of Manifesting.*

Goddard, Neville. *Out of this World. Thinking Fourth-Dimensionally.*

Hamilton, James Roger. *Wealth Dynamics E-Guide.* 2017. Kindle Edition.

Hartmann, Silvia (Dr.). *Adventures in EFT.*

Hill, Napoleon. *Outwitting the Devil.*

Kyne, Peter B. *The Go-Getter.*

Morter, Ted Jr. (Dr.), *Dynamic Health. Using your Own Beliefs, Thoughts and Memory to Create a Healthy Body.*

Patent, Arnold M. *You Can Have It All.*

Proctor, Bob. *You Were Born Rich.*

Robbins, Tony. *Awaken the Giant Within. How to Take Immediate Control of your Mental, Emotional, Physical and Financial Destiny*!

Selacia. *Your Guide to Earth's Pivotal Years. A Direct Path to Enlightened Living.*

Yates, Brad. *The EFT Wizard's Big Book of Tapping Scripts.* Kindle Edition.

Csikszentmihalyi, Michael. *Flow*: *The Psychology of Optimal Experience.*

***

DIGITAL REFERENCES

The Way of the Wizard, Deepak Chopra.
https://www.youtube.com/watch?v=IyMfuTzSDLw

Four Levels of Consciousness.
https://findliaison.com/levels-of-consciousness/

How Long Does It Actually Take to Form a New Habit, James Clear

https://jamesclear.com/habits4

Listen to Life's Whispers, Oprah Winfrey

https://www.youtube.com/watch?v=ki6X6iPeGi

Aadil Palkhivala Wants Yoga to Be More About Integrity and Less About Ego, Aadil Palkhivala

https://www.yogajournal.com/yoga-101/meet-your-next-teacher-aadil-palkhivala

DNA and Soul Purpose. Selacia.
https://spiritlibrary.com/selacia/dna-and-your-soul-purpose-star-seeds-remembering

Ted Talks. www.ted.com/talks

Wealth Trigger Audio Programs, Dr. Joe Vitale and Dr. Steve G. Jones

The Strangest Secret, Earl Nightingale.

https://www.youtube.com/watch?v=m9PmuAFsQOM

University of Toronto. https://www.utoronto.ca/news/u-t-among-top-25-global-universities-academic-research-rankings-shanghai-ranking-consultancy

Spirituality Belongs in Business, Huffington Post, Suzanne West.

https://www.huffingtonpost.com/suzanne-west/spirituality-belongs-in-b_b_10709404.html

Left Brain. Right Brain. Whole Brain. E. Paul Zehr Ph.D.

https://www.psychologytoday.com/us/blog/black-belt-brain/201312/left-brain-right-brain-whole-brain

You're the Average of the Five People You Spend the Most Time With, Jim Rohn, Aimee Groth. https://www.businessinsider.com/jim-rohn-youre-the-average-of-the-five-people-you-spend-the-most-time-with-2012-7

The Meyers-Briggs Type Indicator (MBTI) Personality Test: https://www.opp.com/en/tools/MBTI/MBTI-personality-Types

The Unconquerable, William Ernest Henley https://www.poetryfoundation.org/articles/68606/spiritual-poetry

Maslow's Hierarchy of Needs, Saul McLeod.

https://www.simplypsychology.org/simplypsychology.org-Maslows-Hierarchy-of-Needs.pdf

Be Happy. http://www.behappy101.com/happiness-101.html

The Bio-Energetic Synchronization Technique (B.E.S.T.). https://chiropractor-plantation.com/services/b.e.s.t.html

Map of Consciousness, David. R. Hawkins

https://i.redd.it/0couoapjc8ay.png

Visionary Leadership, Corrine McLaughlin. www.visionarylead.org

Spirituality and Ethics in Business, Corrine McLaughlin. http://www.visionarylead.org/spirituality-in-business.html

How to and Where to Tap your Meridian Points to Reduce Nervousness & Anxiety, Amara Christi, https://www.collective-evolution.com/2015/09/22/surefire-techniques-to-help-you-prepare-for-a-big-event-meeting-or-presentation/

Tapping Therapy, http://www.rogercallahan.com/tapping-therapy.php

Tap with Brad, http://tapwithbrad.com

The Tapping Solution, www.thetappingsolution.com

Spirit Library, www.spiritlibrary.com

***

Appendix B: Relevant Trivia

It takes 68 seconds of focus for a thought to stick and start manifesting in the physical world.

Fourteen (14) seconds of focus equals 2000 hours of activity. Twenty-eight (28) seconds equals 20,000 hours of activity (Jerry & Esther Hicks).

It takes about 30 days to build a new habit and about 66 days for the new behavior to be fully anchored. It takes about 32 days for your brain chemistry to change and for new neuropathways to develop.

Success is a decision away! But once you decide, you have to act within 48 hours after making your decision. This timeframe has to be respected so that supporting neuropathways are formed in your brain. What's the exact science? Within 48 hours after you decide to do X or Y, your brain creates a chemical response to back up your decision. If you do not act within this timeframe, you create a fog of incompletion and are thrown into a state of paralysis.

Choose your company wisely! Your net worth in five years will equal the average of the total net worth of your five closest friends or people that you spend most of your time with.

Subconscious: For every memory in your conscious mind, there is 1 million memories in your subconscious.

Healing Music: Music based on 432Hz frequency transmits beneficial healing energy (i.e. baroque). Classical music therapy nudges us into a slight hypnosis state and brings our brain cells to a state of equilibrium.

Fear: 14,000 known chemical reactions occur in your body when you are in fear.

Rest: You need 10-20 minutes of complete downtime for every 90 minutes of activity in order to function effectively.

Strategy: The Millionaire's Ratio. Focus on the 20% of key things that give you the 80% of outcomes. There is often the top 20% of key priorities that deliver the 80% of results.

Happy people live on average 9 years longer than unhappy people.

***

Appendix C: Success-Building Affirmations

I am alive! I am alert! I feel great!

Day by day, in every way, I am getting better and better!

Day by day, I am becoming more successful!

I am successful and continue to increase my success!

I am wealth! I am abundance! I am joy!

I am focused and believe in myself!

I am a winner! I am a champion!

I am fearless and achieve every goal I set for myself!

I feel happy, I feel fine, I feel like that all the time!

Money comes to me easily, freely and in abundance!

Dollars want me!

I know that I am spiritually perfect!

I love and fully accept myself!

I am grateful for this very moment!

It is my destiny to be successful!

I am breathing in worthiness!

I keep setting new more ambitious goals for myself!

I am somebody!

Everything always works out for me!

I can be, do and have anything and everything that I have ever wanted!

I succeed in everything I do!

I am always at the right place at the right time!

I speak with force and conviction!

My word is my bond! When I say something, I do it!

I am happy, healthy, alive and alert!

I am grateful! I am thankful! I am appreciative!

I have energy pulsating through me!

It's like me to be abundant!

It's like me to be a winner!

That's the new me! That's the way I am now!

I am worthy of receiving information intuitively!

My intuition guides me to prosperity!

I enjoy a deep connection with my intuition!

I am thankful for my gift of intuition!

I make more money when I use my intuition!

My clear intuitive sight allows me to see a clear path to prosperity!

I use my intuition for the greater good!

I am highly intuitive!

I use intuition as if it were another sense!

I am an intuitive wealth builder!

My intuition is directly connected to my desires!

I prosper where ever my intuitive guidance leads me!

My frequency aligns with that of wealth and success!

I communicate my intentions to the universe!

I visualize my success and wealth!

I easily remove obstacles!

I am motivated to attract wealth into my life!

I welcome money into my life now!

I examine opportunities for wealth now!

I build momentum for triggering wealth!

I align my thoughts with positivity and confidence!

I enjoy my wealth and success!

I strive for continuous improvement!

I sustain short and long-term change!

My vibrations are in tune with the universe!

My wealth desires reverberate throughout the universe!

I let go of limiting wealth beliefs!

I feel empowered by what the future holds for me!

I am ready to make changes in my life!

I am a money magnet!

I create a vision for change!

I attract money from a variety of sources!

I commit myself to the pursuit of wealth!

I communicate my wealth vision often!

I choose to feel empowered every day!

I support my own wealth goals!

I am the leader of my life!

I liberate myself from doubt and fears!

I realize that having money is something to be proud of!

The more I make, the more I give!

The more I give, the more I make!

The more I spend, the more abundance comes to me!

The more useful service I render, the more I benefit financially!

I look at my wealth growing and see all the good that will come of it!

I find uplifting wealth opportunities!

My vibration takes me to new levels of success and abundance!

My bravery takes me to new levels of success!

I am an important person!

I have a very well-trained memory!

I move in the direction of happiness and abundance with every step I make!

I am learning how to be, do and have everything I want!

I know how to be, do and have everything I want.

I am powerful! I am influential! I am significant!

I enjoyed reading this book and value the information it contains!

Let the energy of light, love and truth prevail on Earth!

***

Appendix D: Tapping for Specific Issues

Corrections of **Psychological Reversal**: Tap side of the hand (karate spot) or under nose

Drainage of toxins: Tap the collar bone meridian

Fear: Tap side of hand and think of the issue while saying out loud: "I fully love and accept myself".

Visualization of **peak performance**: Tap the under-arm and collar-bone meridian and visualize yourself performing brilliantly

Bonus Tip: The original Bach flower rescue remedy! This product is made out of essences of different flowers and corrects several layers of reversal. It is a natural stress reliever and an excellent protection while travelling. You can easily find it in most health-food stores.

***

Appendix E: Energy Points: Meridians

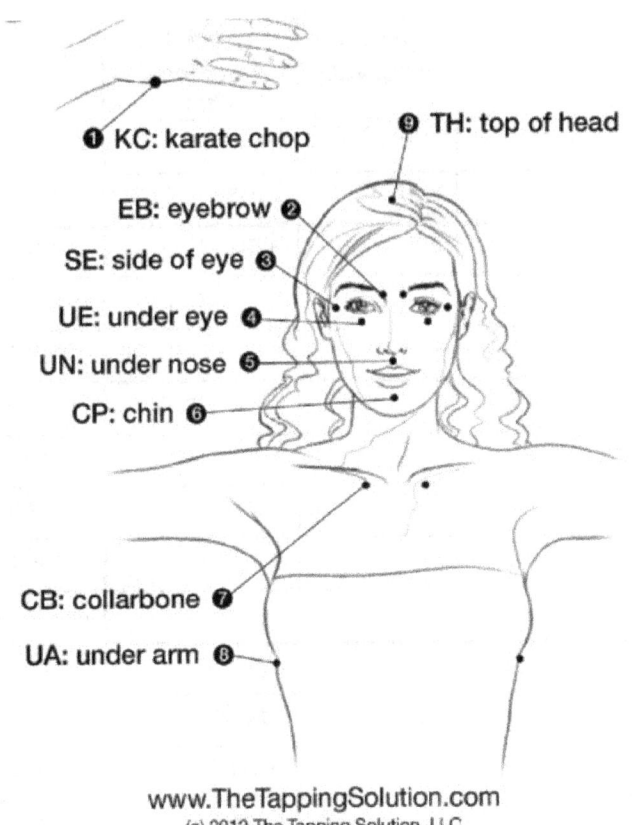

Appendix F: Map of Consciousness

Name of Level	Energetic Frequency	Associated Emotional State	View of Life
Enlightenment	700-1000	Ineffable	Is
Peace	600	Bliss	Perfect
Joy	540	Serenity	Complete
Love	500	Reverence	Benign
Reason	400	Understanding	Meaningful
Acceptance	350	Forgiveness	Harmonious
Willingness	310	Optimism	Hopeful
Neutrality	250	Trust	Satisfactory
Courage	200	Affirmation	Feasible
Pride	175	Scorn	Demanding
Anger	150	Hate	Antagonistic
Desire	125	Craving	Disappointing
Fear	100	Anxiety	Frightening
Grief	75	Regret	Tragic
Apathy	50	Despair	Hopeless
Guilt	30	Blame	Evil
Shame	20	Humiliation	Miserable

Appendix G: Maslow's Hierarchy of Needs

V. Self-actualization

IV. Esteem needs: prestige and feeling of accomplishment

III. Belongingness & love needs: intimate relationships, friends

II. Safety needs: security, safety

I. Physiological needs: food, water, rest, warmth

Note: Group I and II represent our **basic needs**. Group III and IV represent our **psychological needs**. Group V represents our **self-fulfillment** needs, which include the achievement of our full potential and creative activities.

Connect with Me

If you enjoyed this book, connect with me on social media. It would be great to have you join my online community! You can also leave a review with your book retailer.

Follow me on Instagram #TheSpiritualMBA for more success and happiness tips.

Visit my website at www.thespiritualmba.com for a free copy of the *Dollars Want Me* essay.

Until Next Time!

***

The Spiritual MBA

***

SUCCESS TRIGGER PAGE - READING NOTES